The English Garden

The English Garden presents 100 seminal gardens from the Renaissance to the present day. The selection ranges from the formal gardens of the Elizabethan period and the pastoral idylls of the English landscape era, to the herbaceous borders of the early twentieth century and today's cutting-edge designs, embracing form, texture and colour. Organized chronologically, all types and styles are featured, including the ornamental parterre, the botanic garden, the picturesque Arts and Crafts garden, grottoes, Modernist landscapes and innovative, contemporary creations. This book presents the most influential designers, horticulturalists and patrons through their best-known gardens, such as Capability Brown's Blenheim Palace, Gertrude Jekyll's Munstead Wood, Christopher Lloyd's Great Dixter and Piet Oudolf's Millennium Garden at Pensthorpe Waterfowl Park. Explore England's best-loved gardens, from Hampton Court to the Eden Project, alongside lesser-known treasures like Derek Jarman's Prospect Cottage.

The English Garden is an inspiring guide to a nation's passion — the garden.

Moorhouse Sir Thomas More

This is one of the clearest illustrations of a Tudor garden in existence. It forms the background to a miniature portrait of Sir Thomas More and his family, painted by Rowland Lockey in the 1590s, a version of the Holbein original. Brick walls form a square enclosure incorporating on one side a covered gallery and what was possibly a chapel. A low clipped hedge surrounds an asymmetrical series of clipped hedges that form little squares, with several trees planted among them. Little care appears to have been taken to make the design geometrically rigorous, and there are none of the heraldic beasts on gilded poles illustrated in contemporary pictures of the royal gardens of Henry VIII.

Yet this is an example of an early — and modest — knot garden. A gateway gives on to the fields of Chelsea and, presumably, the Thames. It is not known whether More had a hand in the garden's design, but this portion of his estate was gifted to a daughter and son-in-law at his death.

Moorhouse, Chelsea, London, 1520–35, depicted by Rowland Lockey, c1593–4. **Sir Thomas More. b** London, 1478. **d** London, 1535.

Montacute House Sir Edward Phelips

This exquisitely beautiful building was part of the original design for the gardens of Montacute House, created for Sir Edward Phelips during the 1590s. The pavilion, or banqueting house, was one of a pair of garden buildings where guests repaired for desserts and refreshments after dining in the main house. The strong Elizabethan ground plan remains, but within it are flower borders dating from around 1951 that were designed by Mrs Phyllis Reiss, who lived at nearby Tintinhull House and also created the gardens there. The clear, strong colours and large groups of foliage plants provide interest throughout the year. The borders are packed with clematis, vines, roses, delphiniums and lupins during the summer. The north garden was relaid by Graham Stuart Thomas, inspired by Vita Sackville-West, in 1945. The west drive has an avenue of clipped Irish yews, Lebanon cedars and beeches, leading to the new front entrance of the house.

Montacute House, Montacute, Yeovil, Somerset, c1590. **Sir Edward Phelips**. **b** UK, c1555. **d** London, 1614.

Enstone Thomas Bushell

Reached through a watery curtain, this underground cave hung with stalactites displays Thomas Bushell's marvellous hydraulic effects that were accompanied by artificial thunder, lightning, rain, hail, drum-beats, bird-song, lights, rainbows and sounds of the dead arising. One-time page and secretary to philosopher-statesman Sir Francis Bacon,

Bushell came to Enstone in around 1625, living in a small house where he draped his study in black like a melancholy hermitage. In his upper garden were walks, groves, flower gardens and *giochi d'acqua* (water jokes), which were added to after his death. Fame came briefly when he was twice visited by Charles I, but he left Enstone at the start of

the Civil War and never returned. The 'Enstone Marvels', as the gardens were known, were influenced by the Ancient Greek inventor Hero of Alexandria (1st century AD) and the water toys and jokes of European gardens, such as the Italian Villa d'Este and the Austrian Schloss Hellbrunn.

Enstone, Enstone, Chipping Norton, Oxfordshire, c1625, as depicted in *Natural History of Oxfordshire*, Robert Plot, 1677. **Thomas Bushell. b** Worcestershire, 1594. **d** London, 1674.   6

Arundel House Inigo Jones

The English architect Inigo Jones remodelled Arundel House and grounds between 1615 and 1625, providing a gallery wing, which gave onto a walled garden laid out with gates. This appears in the background of this portrait of the Countess of Arundel. His introduction of formal gateways between different gardens was an innovation and his adoption of the garden gate as the boundary between tamed and untamed nature was a distinctive contribution to garden architecture. The novelty of Jones's design also lay in its richly textured rustication and the purity of its Classical detail, as in the courtyard and garden gates. His unaffected style can be seen in the simple arch visible at the far end of the garden. Topped with coping and ball finials, it is set into the full-height flanking walls surrounding the garden. Jones's fantastical stage-set designs, often Italianate in inspiration, were an important influence on contemporary garden design.

Arundel House, The Strand, London, 1615–25, as depicted in *Alathea, Countess of Arundel and Surrey*, Daniel Mytens, c1618. **Inigo Jones**. b London, 1573. d London, 1652.

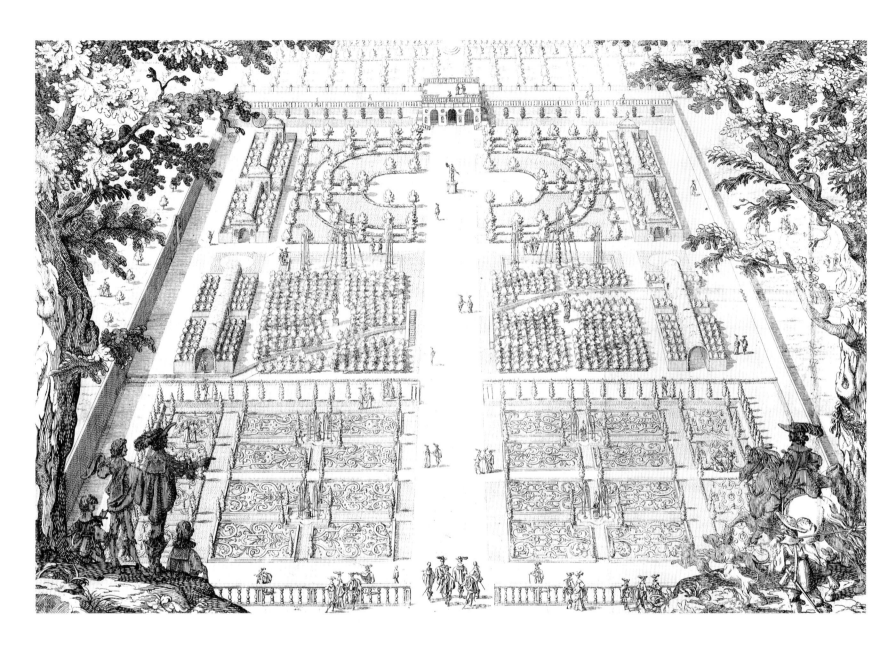

Wilton House *Philip Herbert, 4th Earl of Pembroke*

This engraving of 1645 depicts the garden at Wilton House. Built between 1632 and 1635 around a central axis, it featured terraces, elaborate parterres, a wilderness, water features, statuary, a grotto and galleries. It became famous across Europe as a symbol of the civilization and eclecticism of the Caroline Court in the years before the

Civil War. The garden was designed by Philip Herbert, 4th Earl of Pembroke, with help from Isaac de Caus working with the architect Inigo Jones. The layout was strongly influenced by the villa gardens of the Venetian countryside, which were built on similarly flat sites. It also draws on other European Renaissance gardens, notably the Palais du

Luxembourg in France, which the earl had seen when he escorted Henrietta Maria (wife of Charles I) back to England in 1625. Wilton was particularly important, for it inspired other mid-seventeenth-century English Renaissance gardens such as Dawley, Haigh and Staunton Harold.

Wilton House, Wilton, Salisbury, Wiltshire, 1632–5, as depicted in an engraving of 1645. **Philip Herbert, 4th Earl of Pembroke**. b Wilton, Salisbury, Wiltshire, 1584. d London, 1650.

Hampton Court Henry Wise

This view shows Hampton Court Palace as it was soon after Henry Wise, as royal gardener to King William III, took charge in 1699. The Great Fountain Garden in the foreground, with thirteen fountains and complex *parterres de broderie*, had been laid out by Daniel Marot, and the Privy Garden (top left) had just been finished, possibly with input from Wise and George London, his partner at the Brompton Road Nursery. Wise made several improvements at Hampton Court, including the famous maze, but the most radical changes followed the accession, in 1702, of Queen Anne, who ordered the removal of the box hedges, parterres and most of the fountains. Wise was the leading designer in England in the late seventeenth century, responsible for major works at Blenheim, Castle Howard and Longleat. Almost all his gardens were erased when the mid-eighteenth-century fashion for landscapes in the style popularized by Capability Brown dictated expanses of smooth pasture rather than formal parterres.

Hampton Court Palace, East Molesey, Surrey, 1699–1728. **Henry Wise**. b Oxford, 1653. d Warwick, 1738.

Hanbury Hall George London

The recently restored sunken parterre garden at Hanbury Hall is a fine example of the Dutch-inspired formal style that dominated English garden design at the end of the seventeenth century. Designed by George London and his partner Henry Wise, the sunken garden proves that this style did not have to be austere or impersonal. The restoration was based on a plan of 1732. A choice of brightly coloured plants such as marigolds, lavender, pinks, stocks, tulips and iris, all of them available in the eighteenth century, create a riotous summer display best viewed from the red-brick Long Gallery, which ornaments one raised corner of the quartered parterre. London appears to have worked alone here, and the fruit garden beyond the parterre, with two small trellis pavilions amid apple trees and standard redcurrants and gooseberries in the borders, is a reflection of his horticultural expertise.

Hanbury Hall, Hanbury, Droitwich Spa, Worcestershire, 1701. George London. b 1681. d London, 1714.

Westbury Court Maynard Colchester

Bordered by a hedge, the long canal reflects the tall, slim and elegant summerhouse or gazebo, the dominant feature in this compact garden built between 1694 and 1705. The building's architecture and the surrounding garden reflect a strong Dutch influence. The hedges are topped with 'Dutch topiary', a style in which different evergreens are grown

through the top of the yew hedge and clipped into geometric shapes, here cones and balls. Colchester covered the garden walls with many different types of fruit tree, and filled the parterre garden with thousands of bulbs imported from Holland. This intimate and intricately planted style had become popular when William and Mary

ascended the English throne in 1689, and wars with France ensured that the grandiose French style fell from fashion. Maynard's nephew, also Maynard, continued to develop the garden in the same vein between 1715 and 1756, although by this time it was completely at odds with the prevailing trend, the English landscape garden.

Westbury Court Garden, Westbury-on-Severn, Gloucestershire, 1694–1705, restored from 1971. **Maynard Colchester**. Active UK, late seventeenth and early eighteenth centuries. d 1715.

Levens Hall Guillaume Beaumont

The parterre at Levens Hall is celebrated for its magnificent collection of topiaried yews clipped into an amazing array of shapes. The park and garden, which were influenced by the formal French tradition, were laid out by Beaumont between 1689 and 1712 for Colonel James Grahme, who had been Privy Purse and Keeper of the Buckhounds to James II before the king fled the country in 1688. Beaumont planted great beech and yew hedges to divide the garden into five 'quarters'. These were the orchard, bowling green, soft-fruit garden, the 'mellion-ground' with hot beds and heated frames, and the box-edged parterres with their formal beds and topiary, which are now much larger than would have originally been intended. It is not known whether the designs are based on originals or are entirely the innovations of Alexander Forbes, head gardener from 1810 to 1862, who restored much of the garden and added the golden yew topiary. Beaumont's plan of the gardens is also notable for its very early ha-ha and great bastion.

Levens Hall & Gardens, Kendal, Cumbria, 1689–1712. Guillaume Beaumont. b France, 1650. d Cumbria, 1729.

Claremont Landscape Garden Charles Bridgeman

A Cedar of Lebanon casts its shadow across Bridgeman's great turf amphitheatre which tilts its eight circular terraces (four concave, four convex) like a giant saucer, following the Classical example. Cut into rising ground above the lake (then a formal round pond), the amphitheatre was created c1725 for its landscape drama rather than real

theatre. It also gave fine views across the valley. Once owned by architect Sir John Vanbrugh, Claremont's successive developments tell the story of the English landscape garden. William Kent loosened the reins of Bridgeman's formal landscape, adding a cascade (now a grotto) and ruffling the pond into a more 'natural' lake.

Capability Brown built a new house and hid the amphitheatre under trees. Planted with rhododendrons and exotics, the gardens later became a favourite retreat for Queen Victoria. Bridgeman was appointed gardener to George II and Queen Caroline. His work heralded the new landscape style, but regrettably few of his gardens survive.

Claremont Landscape Garden, Esher, Surrey, begun 1715. Charles Bridgeman. d London, 1738.

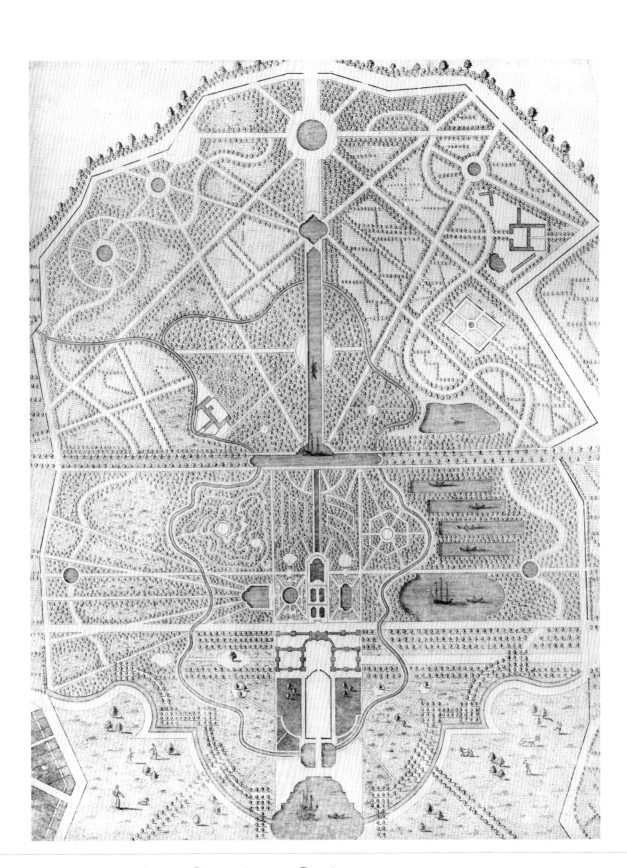

Ichnographia Rustica Stephen Switzer

This illustration from Switzer's book *Ichnographia Rustica* (1718) clearly demonstrates the author's commitment to creating a relationship between the garden and the surrounding landscape, as well as his respect for the Classical tradition of design. He gave this approach the title 'Rural Gardening'. Switzer did not believe in garden walls; he thought that 'all the adjacent country should be laid open to view'. Clearly visible on the plan is the main axis, on which lies the house — an Italian Renaissance idea — and a long canal — an idea drawn from the French Renaissance tradition. The cross-axis also centres on the canal. Switzer saw the use of such long axes as imperative in linking the house to the garden. Crucially, however, the straight *allées* flow into serpentine walks in the outer reaches of the design. Switzer was apprenticed to George London and Henry Wise, and worked alongside Charles Bridgeman as a superintendent at Blenheim.

Illustration from *Ichnographia Rustica*, 1718. **Stephen Switzer. b** Hampshire, 1682. **d** London, 1745.

14

Castle Howard Sir John Vanbrugh

Vanbrugh's Temple of the Four Winds (completed in 1728 after his death) slips heroically into the wild, romantic Yorkshire landscape, offering a distant prospect of Nicholas Hawksmoor's mausoleum and the later 'Roman bridge'. Inspired by Andrea Palladio's Villa Capra near Vicenza, the temple creates harmony by combining the circle and the square. Vanbrugh came to Castle Howard in 1699, fresh from success as a playwright (and earlier imprisonment in the Bastille on suspicion of spying). Working closely with his patron and friend the 3rd Earl of Carlisle, and assisted by Hawksmoor, Vanbrugh added drama to the landscape with his striking buildings that included mock-medieval curtain walls strung with towers and bastions, obelisks and pyramids. Though he never designed gardens himself, Vanbrugh's great talent was for 'composing' his buildings in the landscape like a painter, stimulating the imagination of owners and landscape gardeners like Viscount Cobham at Stowe and Charles Bridgeman at Claremont.

Castle Howard, York, North Yorkshire, 1699–1726. Sir John Vanbrugh. b London, 1664. d London, 1726.

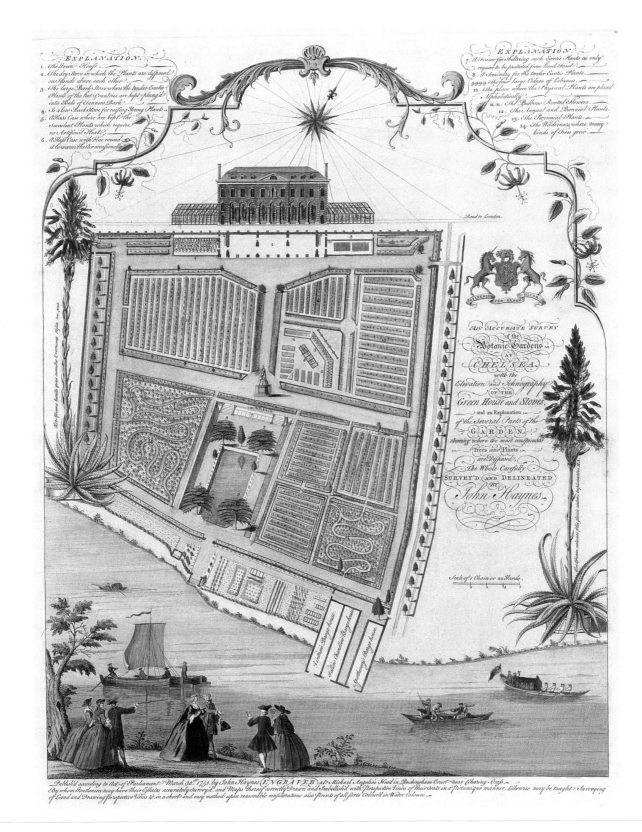

Chelsea Physic Garden Sir Hans Sloane

This plan shows an attractive arrangement of rectangular beds, which would have held collections of plants gathered together by their medicinal use, or as part of a pre-Linnean (Latin) classification system. The garden was established in 1673 by the Society of Apothecaries for the purpose of teaching students the pharmacological uses of different plants, hence the name 'Physic'. In 1722 the garden was rescued from its financial difficulties by the generous patronage of Sir Hans Sloane, physician to George I and plant collector, who had bought the Manor of Chelsea from Lord Cheyne in 1712. Sloane also installed as curator Philip Miller, whose dedication ensured that it became the most richly stocked botanic garden in the world. One plant in the garden, *Sophora microphylla*, is a direct descendant of the original introduction, grown from seed brought back from New Zealand by Sir Joseph Banks, another great patron of the garden. The current layout dates from the late nineteenth century.

Chelsea Physic Garden, Chelsea, London, established 1673, restored 1722, as depicted in an engraving by John Haynes, 1751. **Sir Hans Sloane**. **b** Ireland, 1660. **d** UK, 1753.

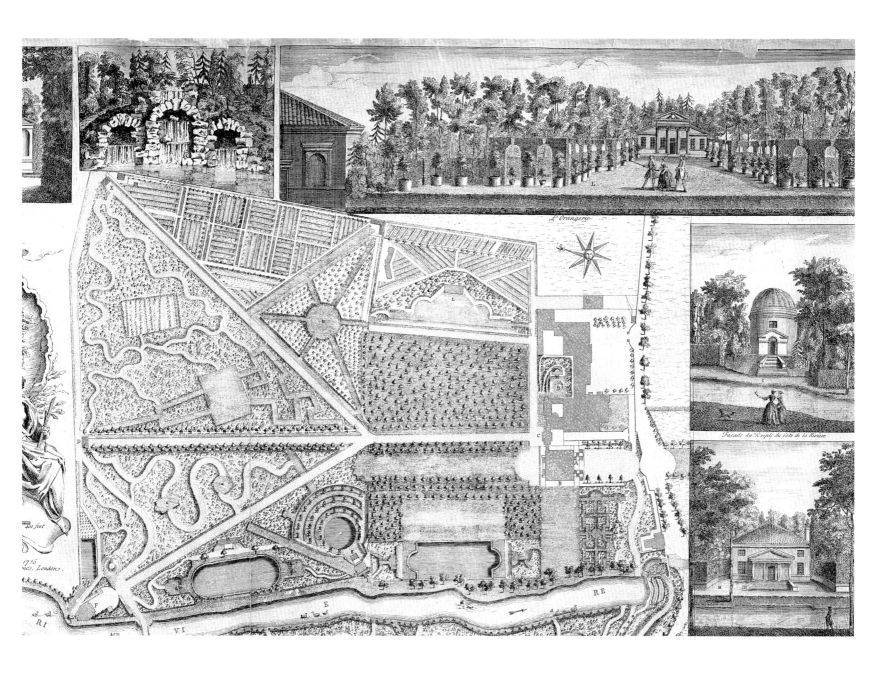

Chiswick House Lord Burlington

John Rocque's 1736 map highlights the irregular winding paths, strong axial layout and natural areas favoured by Lord Burlington, following his Grand Tour, as characteristic of ancient Classical gardens. In contrast to the Baroque formality of earlier gardens, Chiswick House, modelled on Palladio's Villa Rotonda, was set in grounds landscaped by Charles Bridgeman and William Kent, and was at the forefront of fashionable taste. Its features included a river, grotto cascade, hedged exedra with statues (said to be from Hadrian's Villa), banqueting house and pool with an obelisk, some shown in the vignettes bordering the map. Dominant is the *patte d'oie*, with clipped hedges, each of the three vistas culminating in a Classical garden building. Burlington's ideas on the natural style of gardening were immortalized by Alexander Pope in the poem *Epistle to Lord Burlington* (1734), which praised his pioneering work, and advised designers to 'consult the genius of the place'.

Chiswick House and Gardens, Chiswick, London, from 1725, as depicted in an engraving by John Rocque, 1736. **Richard Boyle, 3rd Earl of Burlington**. b London, 1695. d London, 1753.

Bramham Park Robert Benson, 1st Lord Bingley

The Gothic Temple at Bramham Park is an exquisite garden building seen in context, perfectly scaled and at ease in its setting. The garden was created by Robert Benson (later Lord Bingley) in the French formal style of Le Nôtre, with *allées* of high beech hedges, a series of formal pools linked by a cascade and a T-shaped canal. It was later embellished by Benson's descendants. The Gothic Temple was added in 1750 by Harriet Benson, Lord Bingley's daughter, based on a pattern-book design in Batty Langley's *Gothic Architecture* (1742). This is an exhilarating, spacious garden of wide open spaces and long, narrow vistas, ornamented with obelisks, ponds and a variety of temples that command wide views. It is a unique and successful fusion of French formal and English landscape features, with perhaps a touch of the Italian Renaissance in the formal set-pieces, too: an example of the panache and confidence of English garden-making in the early eighteenth century.

Bramham Park, Wetherby, West Yorkshire, 1699–1731. **Robert Benson, 1st Lord Bingley**. **b** Wrenthorpe, Yorkshire, 1675. **d** 1731.

Woburn Farm Philip Southcote

In 1712 Joseph Addison had enjoined landowners to embellish their estates, so 'a Man might make a pretty landskip of his own Possessions', and in the 1730s Philip Southcote was in a position to follow the advice literally. The happy intermixing of practical farming and landscape gardening was an essential tenet of the early landscape movement. At Southcote's influential *ferme ornée* he made a circuit walk of his estate, lined with a flowerbed, 'for convenience as well as pleasure: for from the garden I could see what was doing in the grounds'. He diverted a stream to create a winding waterway and added small garden structures, including a grotto (seen on the right).

Southcote's example caused several gentleman farmers (notably William Shenstone) to decorate their estates similarly, though more modestly. By the late eighteenth century, the *ferme ornée* idea had waned: the only aspects of a working farm Capability Brown allowed in the designed landscape were grazing livestock on decorous pasture.

Woburn Farm, Addlestone, Surrey, from 1735, as depicted in an etching by Luke Sullivan, 1759. **Philip Southcote**. **b** UK, 1698. **d** Witham, Essex, 1758.

Rousham William Kent

A statue of Pan stares pensively across the frosted octagonal pond towards William Kent's serpentine rill. Mist hides the River Cherwell down below, while Venus (unseen) rises from her cascade further up the vale. Remodelled by Kent in 1738 from a more formal design by Charles Bridgeman, Rousham is one of Britain's best preserved (and best loved) early landscape gardens. Horace Walpole likened it to 'Daphne in little, the sweetest little groves, streams, glades, porticos, cascades and river imaginable'. Rousham's 10 hectares (25 acres) should be viewed by following Kent's intended route around the garden. Scenes open up like stage sets, while Classical statues and buildings spark poetic associations. With encouragement from his patron, the 3rd Earl of Burlington (whom he met on his Italian travels), and his friend Alexander Pope, Kent is credited with the notion that 'all nature was a garden'.

Rousham House and Garden, Steeple Aston, Bicester, Oxfordshire, 1738. **William Kent**. **b** Bridlington, Yorkshire, 1685. **d** London, 1748.

Stourhead Henry Hoare II

The Pantheon (1754), a domed rotunda symbolizing the Classical ideal, is glimpsed across a lake, lending a magical aspect to the surrounding landscape. The scene could be from an old master painting, but was the creation of Henry Hoare at Stourhead, his estate in Wiltshire. After the death of his second wife in 1743, Hoare threw himself into the job of improving Stourhead in the most fashionable manner. A large lake was created from a series of ponds formed by the River Stour. Hoare then commissioned Henry Flitcroft, a protégé of Lord Burlington, to add a sequence of exceptionally fine buildings to its perimeter, punctuating a circular walk. Temples to Flora (1745) and Apollo (1765) are well placed and there is a delightful recessed grotto under the lip of the edge of the lake. The scion of a great London banking family, Hoare was closely connected with several early protagonists of the English landscape school, notably Lord Burlington, Alexander Pope and William Kent.

Stourhead, Stourton, Warminster, Wiltshire, from 1743. **Henry Hoare II**. **b** London, 1705. **d** London, 1785.

Studley Royal John Aislabie

A garden composition of abstract beauty, the early eighteenth-century water garden at Studley Royal consists of a lake, a canal and a series of formal ponds that ornament the floor of the steep-sided Skell valley in Yorkshire. Small garden buildings, including a banqueting house by Colen Campbell, adorn the valley sides, creating a variety of vistas. Unlike other early landscape gardens, the natural topography at Studley Royal takes precedence over the designer's architectural impulse, heralding the Picturesque movement later in the century. The climax of the garden, reached via a ride along one edge of the valley, is the surprise view from Anne Boleyn's Seat towards the ruins of medieval Fountains Abbey. Restoration by the National Trust has reinstated a sense of the variety of episodic effects created by John Aislabie to manipulate visitors' emotions.

Studley Royal (Fountains Abbey & Studley Royal Water Garden), Ripon, Harrogate, North Yorkshire, 1693–1742. **John Aislabie**. b nr York, 1670. d Ripon, Harrogate, North Yorkshire, 1742.

Pope's Garden Alexander Pope

The open shellwork temple was a highlight of Alexander Pope's garden, a rectangular 2-hectare (4.8-acre) plot where the poet experimented with painterly techniques of light and shade in his plantings of trees and shrubs, and ornamented the straight *allées*, serpentine paths and glades with Classical urns and statuary. Variety was key,

and the whole scene could be surveyed from a mount. The garden could only be reached from the house via a tunnel under the road, and this Pope converted into a grotto clad with minerals, shells, glass and stalactites literally shot down in Wookey Hole in Somerset. From here a camera obscura view of the Thames, back past the house, could

be enjoyed; it is just visible in the doorway behind the temple in this drawing by William Kent, which shows Kent, Pope and Pope's dog in the garden, as well as fanciful additions such as the sculptural group on the left.

Pope's Garden (Alexander Pope's Grotto), Pope's Villa, Twickenham, Middlesex, 1718–44, as depicted in a drawing by William Kent.
Alexander Pope. b London, 1688. d Twickenham, Middlesex, 1744.

Kew Gardens William Chambers

Across the lake, between the Temples of Victory and Arethusa, William Chambers' ten-storey pagoda rises 49 metres (163 feet) against the sky, a testimony to his venture into Chinoiserie at a period when Chinese style was the prevailing taste in Europe. In 1757 Princess Augusta commissioned Chambers to lay out her garden at Kew, earlier developed as a landscape garden by Capability Brown. Chambers disliked the blandness of Brown's smooth lawns and lakes, preferring gardens that displayed variety — 'the pleasing, the terrible and the surprising'. He filled the garden with more than twenty temples, an aviary, menagerie, mosque, Palladian bridge and the largest hothouse of the time, the Great Stove, illustrated in *Plans of the Gardens and Buildings at Kew* (1763). During this period a small botanic garden was also formed. This garden expanded to become the Royal Botanic Gardens, Kew, with Chambers' pagoda remaining as a reminder of its early history.

Kew Gardens (Royal Botanic Gardens, Kew), Kew, Richmond, Surrey, 1757, depicted in *A View of the Lake and Island at Kew*, Paul Sandby after William Marlowe, 1763. 24
William Chambers. **b** Sweden, 1723. **d** London, 1796.

Rievaulx Terrace Thomas Duncombe

The view from Thomas Duncombe's Rievaulx Terrace is constantly changing — 'a moving variation', Arthur Young called it in 1770. Duncombe laid out the long, spacious terrace near the top of the steep hillside in the 1750s: it curves for more than 1 kilometre (½ mile) between a domed Ionic cupola and a pedimented Tuscan temple; both are banqueting houses. As you walk along the terrace, the views open and shut, so that sometimes the romantic Gothic ruins of the Cistercian Rievaulx Abbey far below are framed by woodland rides and sometimes they disappear altogether. By the time you reach the end, the views of Rievaulx have changed your perception completely. Crucial to Duncombe's scheme is the contrast between the Classical landscape and the sublime decay of the ancient abbey. The terrace represents an important landmark in the history of the English landscape movement, foreshadowing the rise of the Picturesque and renewed antiquarian interest in medieval architecture.

Rievaulx Terrace & Temples, Rievaulx, Helmsley, North Yorkshire, 1758. **Thomas Duncombe**. Active UK, mid-eighteenth century. d UK, 1799.

The Leasowes William Shenstone

This watercolour by the poet and landowner William Shenstone is of the hermitage in his garden, The Leasowes, Halesowen. The figure in the foreground appears to be the hermit himself, a fanciful addition that chimes with the whimsical atmosphere of the place. Shenstone built the garden between 1743 and his death in 1763, on modest means, to ornament the working fields surrounding his farmhouse. It consisted of a varied, circular walk along two wooded combes, relieved by open pastureland, seats and small buildings. It was a solid realization of Shenstone's fanciful verse, evocative of a Classical pastoral idyll. Shenstone posted his own verses, written on pine boards, at strategic points along the garden route. The largest building, the Ruined Priory, was demolished in 1965. For its originality (and the owner's known eccentricity), The Leasowes became one of the most famous and much-visited gardens of the time. It is currently undergoing restoration by the local council.

The Leasowes, Halesowen, West Midlands, 1743–63, as depicted in a watercolour by William Shenstone. **William Shenstone**. b Halesowen, West Midlands, 1714. d Halesowen, West Midlands, 1763.

Painswick Rococo Garden Thomas Robins

The elaborate Rococo border of foliage and shells gives a hint of the unusual attractions of the garden this painting depicts. A figure of Pan greets visitors as they enter the garden; there are long straight vistas and serpentine paths leading around a strange and idiosyncratic collection of buildings, to reveal sudden glimpses of the house and valley below. Robins' painting shares a pictorial convention with the Rococo style of garden design, which exploits the tension between realism and extreme artifice. The garden lies in a valley hidden behind the house, but here the plane of the painting has been tilted in order to give a clear and detailed view. It is thought that Robins, a painter of houses and gardens in the mid-eighteenth century, may also have designed Painswick for owner Benjamin Hyett. It remains the finest and fullest example of a Rococo garden in the country and boasts an exceptional snowdrop display.

Painswick Rococo Garden, Painswick, Stroud, Gloucestershire, 1738–70, as depicted by Thomas Robins. **Thomas Robins**. Active UK, eighteenth century. d UK, c1770.

Downton Castle Richard Payne Knight

Richard Payne Knight started to lay out this intensely dramatic garden in the 1770s, when Capability Brown was at the height of his influence. So different is the scene from gardens in the mid-century English landscape style that it comes as no surprise to learn that Knight was one of Brown's first and most vociferous critics. Knight was a gentleman-designer who set out his views in his poem *The Landscape*, published in 1794. His garden at Downton was cut out of the thickly wooded valley on either side of the River Teme, and included areas of fairly open parkland, but he was keen to create picturesque effects wherever appropriate; this is well exemplified by the two bridges that he suspended across the river. Knight and other advocates of the Picturesque tried to create a frisson of danger in visitors to their gardens. It was the lack of variety in Brown's landscapes that Knight so deplored: '… wrapt all o'er in everlasting green, [it] makes one dull vapid, smooth and tranquil scene.'

Downton Castle, Ludlow, Herefordshire, 1770s. **Richard Payne Knight**. b Wormsley Grange, Herefordshire, 1751. d London, 1824.

Painshill Park Charles Hamilton

Illusion, atmosphere and poetry combine in this tiny Gothic temple (both eyecatcher and viewpoint), mirrored in the still waters of Painshill's artificial lake. From 1738 until his near-bankruptcy in 1773, Hamilton transformed his 80 hectares (200 acres) of barren heath into an earthly paradise, entirely separate from his modest house. One of the eighteenth century's great amateur landscapers, Hamilton manipulated scenes like a painter and theatre designer, introducing many new conifers and shrubs from North America and planting for mood: colourful flowers for the Temple of Bacchus, gloomy yews for the mausoleum. Ever the showman, he hired a duplicitous 'hermit' for his hermitage and instructed his gardener to switch on the waterworks when visitors entered his magical rockwork-and-crystal grotto. His garden's fame was celebrated in sketches by William Gilpin and on Catherine the Great's Wedgwood dinner service. Something of his spirit has driven Painshill's painstaking restoration.

Painshill Park, Cobham, Surrey, 1738–73. **Charles Hamilton**. b Dublin, Ireland, 1704. d Bath, Avon, 1786.

Blenheim Palace Capability Brown

The apparently natural features at Blenheim — the lake, undulating sward and clumps of trees — are all man-made, part of the design of Capability Brown, who held a monopoly over English landscape design during the mid to late eighteenth century. Brown's genius was in adapting a successful formula, based on a romantic idea of pastoral England, and having the confidence to shape it to fit different places and different patrons. Brown assessed the 'capabilities' of each situation, hence his nickname. While it is true that he demolished many formal gardens (notably those of George London and Henry Wise) in favour of pastureland right up to the house, Brown was not averse to retaining formal elements where appropriate. However, he had no interest in the symbolic and literary preoccupations of his predecessors: there are no hidden meanings in his work. It is partly the simplicity of his work that makes it attractive.

Blenheim Palace, Woodstock, Oxfordshire, 1764–74. **Capability Brown (Lancelot Brown)**. b Kirkharle, Northumberland, 1716. d London, 1783.

Strawberry Hill Horace Walpole

In 1747 Horace Walpole bought a small villa at Strawberry Hill in Twickenham, just outside London; in subsequent years he transformed it into a Gothic castle. He was initially attracted to the house because he saw the potential for a spectacular view down to the Thames and the 'borrowed' landscape beyond. This picture shows how successful he was in incorporating the house into the 'natural' landscape that he created. As part of this process he planted trees in clumps of four or five in the meadows. The land was protected from the property of neighbouring villas by a series of ha-has. There was also a wide paved terrace around the house and many plants in pots. Walpole grew these in his own nursery, which was also in the grounds. His essay *On Modern Gardening* (1750–70) hails William Kent as the founder of the English Picturesque tradition, citing the painter Claude Lorrain as his inspiration. However, Walpole differed from Kent in preferring to retain avenues and some formality near the house.

Strawberry Hill (Strawberry Hill House), Twickenham, Middlesex, 1747–76. **Horace Walpole**. b London, 1717. d London, 1797.

31

Stowe Landscape Gardens Richard Grenville-Temple

The Corinthian Arch on the great South Vista draws the eye across the Octagon Lake to the horizon. The 18-metre (60-feet) high triumphal arch, which is inhabited, was designed in 1765 for Richard Grenville-Temple (2nd Earl Temple) to complement the new, broader view from the house that had been created by well-placed clumps of trees and the

reconstruction of Vanbrugh's Lake Pavilions at a greater distance apart. Throughout the eighteenth century the Temple family employed leading designers such as Charles Bridgeman, William Kent and Capability Brown to create an idealized Classical landscape, including over thirty temples and monuments, in a style that reflected the contemporary

obsession with ancient Rome and Greece. Three successive generations of the family — Viscount Cobham, 2nd Earl Temple and the Marquess of Buckingham — were influential in transforming the formal seventeenth-century terraces into a naturalistic garden, taken as the model of the English landscape garden throughout the world.

Hawkstone Park Sir Rowland & Sir Richard Hill

This is one of several deep ravines cut out of the rocky landscape at Hawkstone in Shropshire. In order to understand its context, it helps to know that these gloomy chasms are accompanied by dizzying pinnacles, soaring sandstone rocks and ornamental follies, which fill a huge estate, once more than 300 hectares (700 acres). It is the

contrasts that make this landscape unique: the mosses, ferns and dampness of these dark gullies turn suddenly into dramatic cliffs, tunnels, crags and bridges, while the peaks of the precipitous outcrops offer views across thirteen counties. These effects are deliberate — an essential element of the Picturesque movement of which

Hawkstone is one of the best examples: it sought to create contrasts of emotion in the natural landscape. Sir Rowland Hill began the landscaping in the 1750s, but most of what remains was initiated by his bachelor elder son Sir Richard, and completed by his grandson, another Sir Rowland Hill, best known for inventing the postage stamp.

Hawkstone Park, Weston-under-Redcastle, Shrewsbury, Shropshire, c1750–95. **Sir Rowland Hill**. b UK, 1705. d UK, 1783.
Sir Richard Hill. b Hawkstone Park, Weston-under-Redcastle, Shrewsbury, Shropshire, 1733. d Hawkstone Park, Weston-under-Redcastle, Shrewsbury, Shropshire, 1809.

Royal Pavilion John Nash

The building, conceived as a seaside villa for the Prince Regent, was built in 1787, but the remodelling in the Indian-influenced 'Hindu' style that the prince had admired at Sezincote in Gloucestershire, was undertaken by Nash in 1808. Nash had been recommended to the prince by Humphry Repton as the architect for a conservatory — part of the new gardens that Repton had added to the villa in 1797. However, when it came to the remodelling, Nash — who benefited from thirty years of royal patronage — acted in an underhand way. He did not keep his part of the agreement with Repton, and even excluded Repton's plans for the remodelling of the villa that were drawn up in 1808.

Nevertheless, Nash's approach to garden and landscape design was strongly influenced by Repton, and in the limited space of the Pavilion gardens Nash responded to the growing passion for floriculture, designing a series of flowerbeds that were filled with exotic plants by W T Aiton, the superintendent of the Royal Botanic Gardens at Kew.

The Royal Pavilion, Brighton, East Sussex, 1808, redesigned 1815–23. **John Nash**. **b** London, 1752. **d** East Cowes, Isle of Wight, 1835.

Sheringham Park Humphry Repton

Humphry Repton designed both house and garden at Sheringham Park, set in a wooded valley within sight of the sea. After the death of Capability Brown in 1783, Repton saw a career opportunity and successfully took on the mantle of England's foremost landscape designer. In many ways he also inherited Brown's style (on a smaller scale),

creating skilful compositions that exploited the natural topography to form romantic visions of pastoral ease. Repton's main innovation was to reintroduce areas of formality by the house (Brown had pasture right up to the walls): terraces, shrubberies, steps, balustrades and enclosed flower gardens (as at Sheringham). Like Brown,

Repton also had a shrewd commercial eye, and his Red Books — before-and-after views of potential clients' estates, complete with flip-over sections that added lakes or clumps of trees — were an early appeal to the 'makeover' mentality. The house was only partially completed in 1819, after Repton's death in 1818.

Sheringham Park, Upper Sheringham, Norfolk, begun 1812; partially completed 1819. Humphry Repton. b Bury St Edmunds, Suffolk, 1752. d Romford, Essex, 1818.

Alton Towers Thomas Allason & Robert Abraham

A conifer collection provides the backdrop to the pristine gravel paths, which contrast with the manicured lawn and ostentatious display of bedding. Laid out from 1814, and cluttered with many diverse features, including a two-tiered megalith, a three-storeyed cast-iron prospect tower and a Swiss cottage for a blind harper, this romantic valley site

became infamous as the early nineteenth century's most inharmonious garden. Abraham added a series of exotic conservatories and in the late 1820s John Claudius Loudon, the leading garden writer of the day, commented that the garden was 'the work of a morbid imagination joined to the command of unlimited resources'. Perhaps

Allason's greatest influence was to force early Victorian garden designers to think about the congruity of features in the landscape. In the 1840s Alexander Forsyth, the head gardener, planted the conifers and rhododendrons, which introduced a degree of harmony by removing the sharp contrasts between the features.

Alton Towers, Alton, Staffordshire, 1814–27. **Thomas Allason**. b UK, 1790. d UK, 1852. **Robert Abraham**. b London, 1775. d London, 1850.

Westonbirt Arboretum Robert Stayner Holford

The Acer Glade is a sight to wonder at, with its collection of Japanese maples glowing at the peak of their spectacular autumnal foliage display. The arboretum was begun in 1829 when Robert Holford laid out the bones of his grand scheme, a series of radiating rides linked together by informal paths and glades, on his father's estate. It became his life's work; Holford even commissioned plant hunters to bring back new and rare species from abroad. The famous Acer Glade and Colour Circle were planted between 1850 and 1875. Robert's son, George, continued to develop the arboretum, as did Lord Morley (George's nephew) who inherited the estate in 1926. However, five years after his death in 1956, Westonbirt passed to the Crown in lieu of death duties and thence to the Forestry Commission, which has restored, consolidated and maintained this wonderful collection. Today, gathered together within the 242-hectare (600-acre) site are over 18,000 trees.

Tresco Abbey Garden Augustus Smith

Sheltered from Atlantic gales behind a belt of trees, the vast collection of rare, exotic and tender plants imbues the garden with an air of subtropical luxuriance. Augustus Smith, who began the gardens in 1834, terraced the steeply sloping site and introduced paths that wind along the natural contours or plunge steeply downwards. Plants from the southern hemisphere, especially Australasia, are particularly well represented among the collection, which looks very much at home covering the rocky slopes. In many ways, Smith's collector's mentality was typical of the Victorian era, when floral mania gripped the well-to-do, as plant hunters introduced thousands of new species from all around the world. And while Smith gathered plants that thrived in the mild microclimate of Tresco, others collected plants from a particular geographic location, or specific botanical groups — favourites included rhododendrons, conifers, ferns and orchids. After Smith's death, his family continued to care for his philanthropic project.

Tresco Abbey Garden, Tresco, Isles of Scilly, 1834. **Augustus Smith**. b London, 1804. d Plymouth, Devon, 1872.

Scotney Castle William Sawrey Gilpin

From the balustraded terrace, a sweeping view across the autumnal landscape towards the romantic ruins of a turreted castle looks breathtakingly natural. Though the castle is real, the view is entirely manipulated as a last glorious essay in Picturesque gardening by William Sawrey Gilpin, called in by owner Edward Hussey in 1836 to advise on the siting of a new house (by architect Anthony Salvin). Gilpin's advice demonstrated his painter's eye: build the new house high on a bastion and incorporate the old as ruins into the view, obeying the principles of landscape composition with foreground, middle ground and distance. A protégé of Picturesque theorist Sir Uvedale Price, Gilpin came to landscape gardening late (aged fifty-eight) after his career as a painter faltered. He had helped his famous uncle, the Reverend William Gilpin, with illustrations for *Observations on the River Wye* (1782), a Picturesque tour of the River Wye, sparking a whole new sensibility that looked for pictures in the wild landscape.

Scotney Castle, Lamberhurst, Tunbridge Wells, Kent, 1836. **William Sawrey Gilpin**. b UK, 1761/2. d Gilling West, North Yorkshire, 1843.

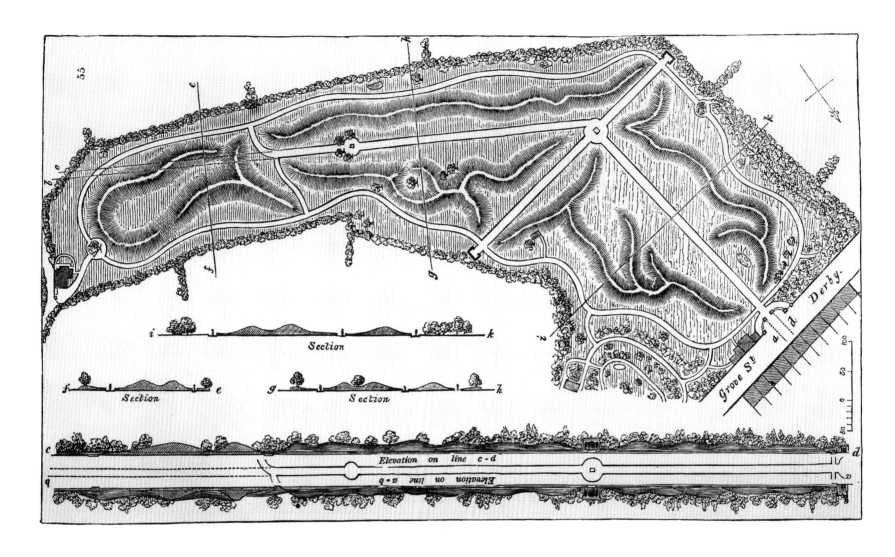

Derby Arboretum John Claudius Loudon

The importance of this plan lies not so much in its layout as in the fact that it was the first large public park to be designed in Britain. The 4.4-hectare (10.5-acre) site was donated to the people of Derby by the philanthropist Joseph Strutt, and opened in September 1840 as a park. Entry to everyone was free for two days each week (including Sundays) and for a moderate charge at other times. Having visited public parks and promenades on his travels to Europe, Loudon had come to see them as an instrument of social reform, a measure 'for promoting the convenience, the good order, and the instruction of the population'. Derby Arboretum was essentially a collection of trees, following in its layout Loudon's principle of the gardenesque. By this method, plants were positioned to best display their individual attributes and, in contrast with the great naturalistic landscapes of the eighteenth century, the hand of man was clearly visible in their arrangement.

Derby Arboretum, Derby, Derbyshire, 1840. **John Claudius Loudon**. b Cambuslang, Lanarkshire, 1783. d London, 1843.

Arley Hall R E Egerton-Warburton

The perfect sward path leading to the Classical seat is flanked on either side by a wide herbaceous border backed by a tall yew hedge. The richly planted borders could be mistaken for late nineteenth-century creations, but in fact they date from the 1840s and are one of the earliest examples of a 'mixed border'. In keeping with the vogue of the time, Egerton-Warburton not only planted the borders in a deliberately anti-Picturesque style that clearly displayed the hand of man, but he also drew inspiration from historic gardens: in this case the enclosed seventeenth-century herb gardens of John Parkinson, Nicholas Culpeper and John Gerard. Although the borders at Arley are an early example, they demonstrate that, contrary to popular myth, the hardy herbaceous perennial did not become extinct when the craze for tender annual and bedding schemes took hold, nor did Gertrude Jekyll 'invent' the herbaceous border. Indeed, from the 1850s onwards these 'old-fashioned' plants acquired romantic poetic associations.

Harewood House Sir Charles Barry

This view represents one of the best examples of an early Victorian garden: you are standing on the steps of Harewood House, looking over Sir Charles Barry's formal Italianate terrace, towards Capability Brown's (1716–83) lake and landscape below. It was quite the fashion in the mid-nineteenth century to insert a formal garden between the house and the 'natural' landscape of the previous century. The terraced formal gardens would be laid out on the Italian model — Italianate rather than Italian — and richly planted with colourful bedding. Barry was one of the leading exponents of this change of fashion, although he is better known for building the Gothic-styled Houses of Parliament in Westminster. Many formal gardens were abandoned in the mid-twentieth century, but Harewood was restored in the 1990s: the outlines of the formal beds are exactly as Barry designed them, though the statue in the centre of the pool is modern.

Harewood House, Harewood, Leeds, West Yorkshire, 1844. **Sir Charles Barry**. **b** London, 1795. **d** London, 1860.

Highnam Court James Pulham

At first glance this garden room seems to be a natural scene made with real rock outcrops, home to that most Victorian of obsessions, a collection of conifer trees. Dating from 1849, it is, however, the first rockery made by James Pulham (son of James Sr, a pioneer in the manufacture of Portland cement) from a mixture of natural stone and 'Pulhamite'. Pulhamite was an artificial rock made by pouring a special mix of Portland cement over a rough structure made of brick and clinker and sculpting it into natural-looking strata. Pulham became so skilful at imitating real rock that it is very difficult to distinguish the reproduction from the genuine article. Pulham's work had a huge impact on the Victorian fashion for creating rock gardens that imitated natural scenes; other famous examples of his work include Sandringham Park in Norfolk and Battersea Park in London. Sadly, the secret recipe for Pulhamite went to the grave with James's son.

Highnam Court Gardens, Highnam, Gloucester, Gloucestershire, 1849. **James Pulham**. b UK, c1820. d UK, 1898.

Rydal Mount William Wordsworth

Built in local slate with interior rustic panelling, William Wordsworth's summerhouse opens to a surprise view of Rydal Water where his extension of the narrow terraces reflects his active style of composing poetry. After the miniature effects of Dove Cottage, where William and sister Dorothy planted native flowers and mosses, his last home

gave Wordsworth scope to indulge his passion for making gardens that blended with the landscape. From 1813 onwards he brought the old kitchen garden into his overall design, and linked the house to its Lakeland setting through terraces, lawns, shrubberies, fields and woodland, planting many evergreens, including a newly introduced

Japanese red cedar (*Cryptomeria japonica*) near the house. An early conservationist, Wordsworth lamented the mass plantations of 'foreign' larch and fir, and praised humble cottage gardens. His romantic, largely vernacular gardening looked forward to William Morris, John Ruskin and William Robinson.

Biddulph Grange James Bateman & Edward W Cooke

A glorious display of foliage is framed by one of the many buildings that grace this garden while, in the distance, another archway beckons you on. In 1849, Cooke, an artist turned garden designer, visited Bateman at Biddulph Grange and over the next decade or so the pair contrived a garden made up of a series of rooms, each home to a different collection of plants. The presence of a pinetum and an arboretum testify to the influence of Chatsworth and Elvaston. The garden rooms were inspired by different aspects of garden history, with names such as 'China', 'Cheshire Cottage' and 'Egyptian Court'. They are graced by an array of stylized garden buildings. One of the finest attributes of Biddulph's design is the way in which the separate rooms are ingeniously linked by a series of effects that constantly surprise and amuse. Biddulph's design was an example of what could be achieved without the need for distant vistas, and the garden was influential in moulding suburban villa gardens.

Biddulph Grange Garden, Biddulph, Staffordshire, c1842–71. **James Bateman**. **b** Redivals, Bury, Lancashire, 1812. **d** Worthing, Sussex, 1897.
Edward W Cooke. **b** London, 1811. **d** Groombridge, East Sussex, 1880.

Chatsworth Sir Joseph Paxton

The Conservative Wall, designed by James Paine and completed in 1763, is one part of previous garden incarnations which Sir Joseph Paxton — working closely with his employer, the 6th Duke of Devonshire (1790–1858) — incorporated into a programme of garden works that began in 1826. Prior to the wall being glazed in 1848, he had begun planting the Arboretum (1835), built the Great Conservatory (1836), erected the huge rockwork (1842) and reconstructed the Weeping Willow Fountain, dating from 1693. The Emperor Fountain (1843) was built for the impending visit of Tsar Nicholas. The gardens at Chatsworth, along with those at Biddulph Grange, had an enormous impact on Victorian suburban villa garden design. Paxton was one of the most energetic polymaths of the nineteenth century — he was a pioneer of public-park design, an architect, author, engineer and politician. But he is undoubtedly most famous as designer of the Crystal Palace for the 1851 Great Exhibition.

Chatsworth, Bakewell, Derbyshire, 1826–58. **Sir Joseph Paxton**. b Milton Bryan, Buckinghamshire, 1803. d Sydenham, Kent, 1865.

Vauxhall Pleasure Gardens Jonathan Tyers

This stage was built at the centre of the New Spring Gardens in Vauxhall, London. It was used by visitors to the pleasure gardens as a place to drink, feast and watch the crowds walking up and down the *allées*. The gardens were first designed and built in the early to mid-seventeenth century and their principal feature was a series of grand walks and smaller *allées* which cut through a wood of elm and sycamore, intersecting at right angles. This thickly wooded wilderness, where people could choose to be seen or hidden, was the pleasure gardens' main appeal to the public. From the central set, visitors could watch moonlit concerts, alfresco banquets, masquerades, fireworks and spectacles of every conceivable kind. Pleasure gardens continued to exist in England until the end of the nineteenth century but none has survived intact. The Tivoli Gardens in Copenhagen were influenced by Vauxhall.

Belsay Hall Sir Arthur Edward Middleton

Extensive parkland, terraces and a 4.5-metre (14.4-feet) arched ha-ha dropping from the Greek Revival house to the tranquil lake are all the work of Sir Arthur's grandfather, Sir Charles. Behind the lake is the deep, picturesque quarry garden that was developed by Sir Arthur on the site created when stone was extracted to build the house. Following the twin Victorian obsessions of novelty and collecting, Sir Arthur filled the quarry garden with many rare and exotic semi-hardy trees and shrubs. In the mid and late nineteenth century such novelties were pouring into Britain as a result of expeditions made by the plant hunters, but many required the mild growing conditions found in southern Cornwall or the west coast of Scotland. The unusually sheltered conditions within the quarry allowed Sir Arthur to make a collection unique in this northern part of Britain. Inside the quarry a high arch and a secret door marked by tangled branches lure the visitor on. Beyond a narrow passage, a view of the ruined manor is revealed.

Belsay Hall, Castle & Gardens, Belsay, Ponteland, Northumberland, c1870s. **Sir Arthur Edward Middleton**. b UK, 1838. d UK, 1932.

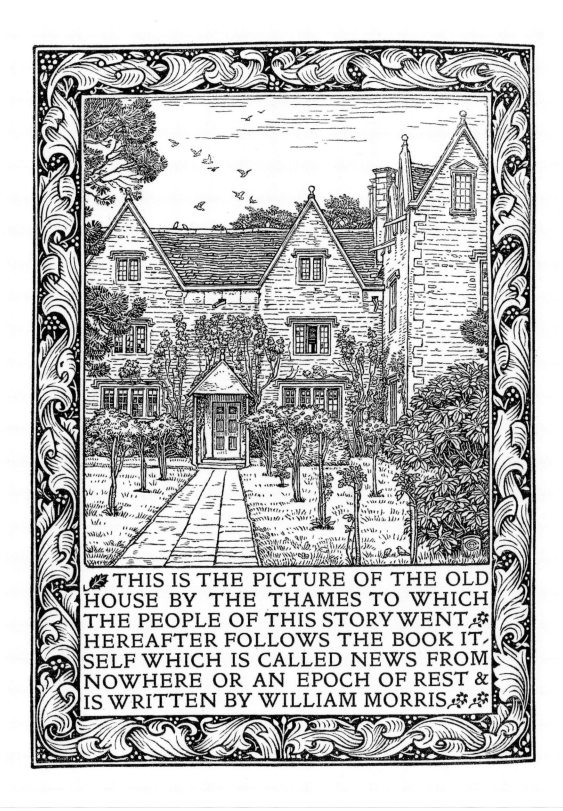

THIS IS THE PICTURE OF THE OLD HOUSE BY THE THAMES TO WHICH THE PEOPLE OF THIS STORY WENT. HEREAFTER FOLLOWS THE BOOK IT.SELF WHICH IS CALLED NEWS FROM NOWHERE OR AN EPOCH OF REST & IS WRITTEN BY WILLIAM MORRIS.

Kelmscott Manor William Morris

A row of standard roses flanks the path that approaches the front door of this lovely Cotswold house. There is such a strong sense of place that both house and garden feel as if they have simply grown out of the ground, rather than been designed. This setting provided William Morris, famous for his textile designs and writings that promoted the revival of the craftsman, with the perfect setting in which he could apply his own dictum that every workman or artist should have an environment in which he or she could lead a creative and satisfying life. Morris, one of the founders and the leading light of the Arts and Crafts movement, thought gardens should have straight paths, ordered rows of vegetables and straight borders from which erupt a riot of flowers that spill over the edges. He found the Cotswolds perfectly suited to his approach, as his comment on another cottage he saw in the village of Broadway in 1876 illustrates: it was 'a work of art and a piece of nature — no less'.

Kelmscott Manor, Kelmscott, Lechlade, Gloucestershire, 1871, depicted in the title page to Morris's *News from Nowhere* (1891). **William Morris**. b London, 1834. d London, 1896.

Brantwood John Ruskin

John Ruskin's local slate seat (specially made by a friend's gardener) turns to face the Lakeland stream rather than Coniston's grander scenery. By closely observing the stream's leaps and pools, Ruskin declared that he could learn as much about the underlying laws of nature as from Niagara's 'vulgar cataracts'. The great Victorian thinker's purchase of Brantwood in 1871 gave him a 'living laboratory' in which to explore his ideas on social welfare, aesthetics and practical land-management. Until the onset of mania, he developed the simple house and 8.4 hectares (21 acres) of craggy rock and coppiced woodland into a cottage villa where he could achieve a sense of rightness and peace. Happiness would come, he believed, 'not by the enlargement of the possessions, but of the heart'. As artist, scientist, philosopher, writer, political radical and pre-eminent art critic, Ruskin straddled the Victorian age, prefiguring the rise of environmentalism. Today Brantwood continues Ruskin's radical experiments in horticulture.

Holkham Hall William Andrews Nesfield

Delicate tracery, laid out in an intricate Louis XIV pattern of box and flower beds against a background of coloured gravels, distinguishes this parterre of the great formal terrace at Holkham, designed by William Andrews Nesfield in 1854. A pool surrounding the statue of Saint George and the Dragon, by R C Smith, can just be seen in front of the sunken panels of this southerly terrace. A further terrace by Nesfield to the north integrates the initials of the owners into the parterre. Nesfield led a revival of interest in this elaborate seventeenth-century art form, creating parterres for country houses. He is also well known for the series of gardens he created for the Royal Botanic Gardens at Kew from 1844 to 1848. His work at Holkham (1849–72) forms part of a long and distinguished tradition of invention; the vast parkland has been transformed by William Kent, Capability Brown and John Webb since the creation of the estate in 1720.

Holkham Hall, Wells-next-the-sea, Norfolk, 1849–72. **William Andrews Nesfield**. b Chester-le-Street, County Durham, 1793. d London, 1881.

Gravetye Manor William Robinson

The formal architecture of the Elizabethan manor is all but hidden by a riot of mixed native and exotic perennials. This triumph of informality over architecture is a perfect cameo of William Robinson's views on garden-making. A prolific author, advocate of woodland gardening, hardy plants and champion of the natural approach, where plants were positioned to best display their individual beauties, Robinson vehemently disliked the High Victorian style of formal flowerbeds. He vitriolically attacked parterres and geometric beds cut into lawns, describing them as 'broken brick' and 'pastry cook' gardening. Robinson also argued that garden design was the realm of gardeners, a stance that brought him into conflict with architects, notably Sir Reginald Blomfield. Blomfield favoured the formal Renaissance style, and saw garden design as a matter for the architect. The matter was resolved when Jekyll and Lutyens demonstrated that gardener and architect could design the garden together.

Gravetye Manor, East Grinstead, West Sussex, 1885. **William Robinson**. b Ireland, 1838. d Gravetye Manor, East Grinstead, West Sussex, 1935.

Wightwick Manor Alfred Parsons

Sizeable groupings of vibrant herbaceous colour complement the high yew walls and Arts and Crafts architecture at Wightwick Manor. Alfred Parsons, a noted watercolourist who provided the illustrations for Ellen Willmott's *The Genus Rosa* (1910–14), was engaged to design a garden with his professional design partner,

Captain Walter Croker St Ives Partridge. He made a self-consciously Old English garden of formal enclosures of yew, embellished with topiary peacocks, flower borders and climbing roses. His scheme included a long yew walk and a rose garden that was later adorned with a grand circular pergola. Parsons' scheme at Wightwick epitomizes Arts

and Crafts gardening, in which careful harmonies and contrasts of flower colour are presented against red-brick architecture and high hedges. The garden is further dignified by the work of Thomas Mawson, who later added terraces, steps and other architectural detailing.

Wightwick Manor, Wightwick Bank, Wolverhampton, West Midlands, 1887. **Alfred Parsons**. b Beckington, Frome, Somerset, 1847. d Broadway, Worcestershire, 1920.

Athelhampton Inigo Thomas

This view of the Great Court garden at Athelhampton, a Victorian reconstruction, is redolent of an imagined Old English gardening style. The tall pyramids of clipped yew enclose an Italianate fountain and are themselves echoed by the shape of the pinnacles on the terrace garden beyond. What it does not tell us is that the entire area around the pool was originally laid out with parterres that were filled with bright bedding in summer and autumn. Inigo Thomas was the architect of the garden and he designed it with such regard for authenticity that it is often mistaken for a seventeenth-century garden rather than a product of the 1890s. Thomas was a proponent of the formal garden, and illustrated Sir Reginald Blomfield's *The Formal Garden in England* (1892). Both helped to create a demand for period gardens to go with Jacobean houses.

Athelhampton House & Gardens, Athelhampton, Dorchester, Dorset, c1890. **Inigo Thomas**. b Yorkshire, 1865. d London, 1950.

Caerhays Castle John Charles Williams

Hidden away from the prevailing south-westerly winds that batter the south Cornish coast, the sheltered gardens not only enjoy a spectacular view, but are also home to an enormous collection of rare trees and shrubs, with a particular emphasis on rhododendrons, magnolias and camellias. The garden was begun in the 1890s, and throughout the early twentieth century John Charles Williams, owner of Caerhays, was a member of various syndicates that sponsored plant hunters such as George Forrest to explore remote parts of China and bring back new plants. Williams also had close ties with the Veitch Nursery at Exeter, and the gardens boast many early introductions from Veitch's plant hunter, Ernest Wilson. However, the gardens are most famous as the birthplace of the *Williamsii* hybrid camellias, created in 1925 when *C. japonica* was crossed with *C. saluenensis*, which had been brought to Britain by Forrest the previous year.

Caerhays Castle Gardens, Gorran, St Austell, Cornwall, 1890s. **John Charles Williams**. b UK, 1862. d UK, 1939.

Myddelton House Edward Augustus Bowles

A pergola, that most Edwardian of features, is underplanted with part of the enormous and eclectic collection of plants that E A Bowles gathered in his 2-hectare (4.8-acre) garden from 1895. Bowles was a leading plantsman of the late nineteenth and early twentieth centuries, and one of a breed of enthusiastic and talented amateurs who helped push forward the science of horticulture. His was a highly individual garden, filled with compartments linked together in a somewhat incoherent way, but boasting many and varied plant species. Enlivened with seasonal bulbs, the Alpine Meadow was surmounted by the famous Rock Garden. Great swathes of irises flanked one bank of the river, while the Stone Garden boasted a fossilized tree, and the Lunatic Asylum consisted of a collection of botanical oddities. Bowles is possibly best remembered for the charming trilogy of books, *My Garden in Spring* (1914), *My Garden in Summer* (1915) and *My Garden in Autumn and Winter* (1915).

Myddelton House Gardens, Enfield, Middlesex, 1895. **Edward Augustus Bowles**. b Myddelton House, Enfield, Middlesex, 1865. d Myddelton House, Enfield, Middlesex, 1954.

Munstead Wood Gertrude Jekyll

Crammed full of herbaceous plants, this border looks artless, and yet it is all due to the designer's skill. Gertrude Jekyll's planting schemes, while profuse and ebullient, were also carefully orchestrated and controlled to achieve exactly the effect she wanted. This photograph was taken during Jekyll's lifetime. As a painter she had spent time in Paris with the Impressionists, but when her eyesight began to fail she dedicated herself to gardening. Jekyll moved into Munstead Wood, a house designed by the architect Sir Edwin Lutyens, in 1897. The 6 hectares (15 acres) of garden were a laboratory in which she experimented with her plant associations and honed her skill of using painterly colour theory in the garden. Jekyll literally used plants as paints and made garden pictures within her borders. Hers was a completely innovative approach to planting, and her partnership with Lutyens created a new English garden style in the Arts and Crafts vernacular.

Munstead Wood Garden, Busbridge, Godalming, Surrey, 1897. **Gertrude Jekyll**. **b** London, 1843. **d** Munstead Wood, Busbridge, Godalming, Surrey, 1932.

Iford Manor Harold Peto

On the far side of the main terrace lies the Casita, with pink marble columns and a Graeco-Roman nymph set into a niche. Clipped box hedges, topiary in pots and a marble figure of a youth fill the foreground. This is not the Italian *campagna* but Iford Manor in Wiltshire, where the English love of the Italian Renaissance garden finds its most

personal expression. Harold Peto gave up his architectural practice to concentrate on garden design. He bought Iford Manor in 1899 and set the garden into the steep, wooded Frome valley with great skill, building a series of terraces with retaining walls of local stone, and incorporating colonnades, loggias and a remarkable

collection of sculptures. Architectural elements are balanced with evergreens, climbers and plants grown between paving. Through a sensitivity to landscape and integration of planting with architecture, he reversed the trend for the grandiose and overly formal Italianate gardens of the Victorians.

Iford Manor (The Peto Garden at Iford Manor), Bradford-on-Avon, Wiltshire, 1899. **Harold Ainsworth Peto**. b London, 1854. d Iford Manor, Bradford-on-Avon, Wiltshire, 1933.

Warley Place Ellen Ann Willmott

The delightfully informal display of foxgloves and Solomon's seal are part of the huge designed collection of common, rare and exotic plants that filled Warley Place. A skilled gardener — many a cultivar or species is named 'Willmott' or 'Warley' — in 1897 Ellen Willmott, along with Gertrude Jekyll, was among the first sixty recipients of the Royal Horticultural Society's Victoria Medal of Honour. She was also a patron of several plant hunters, including Ernest Wilson, and one of the 'levers' Charles Sargent used in order to persuade Wilson to join him at the Arnold Arboretum. If her magnus opus was *The Genus Rosa* (1910–14), she is perhaps better remembered for her popular *Warley Garden in Spring and Summer* (1909). She was one of the first women elected to the Linnean Society (in 1904–5) and 'Miss Willmott's Ghost', a common name for *Eryngium giganteum*, refers either to her habit of surreptitiously sprinkling its seed in gardens she visited, or to her somewhat prickly character.

Godinton Sir Reginald Blomfield

The Italian Garden with its water feature set amid a swath of greensward runs perpendicular to the Walled Garden seen beyond the pergola. It encapsulates how Blomfield, an architect and author of *The Formal Garden in England* (1892), was influenced by the formality of the English Renaissance garden. This 'room' is part of the 12-acre

garden which surrounds the house on three sides. Its architectural shape, structure and materials are typical of Blomfield's work, in which plants were subservient. He saw the garden as a setting for the house and part of the architect's remit, which brought him into conflict with horticulturists, notably William Robinson, who saw garden

design as a gardener's role. These polar views sparked the late nineteenth century 'Battle of Styles', which pitted the formalists against the naturalists, as claimants to the future of garden design. In fact, the outcome was the new Arts and Crafts garden epitomized by the work of gardener and architect — Gertrude Jekyll and Sir Edwin Lutyens.

Godinton House & Gardens, Ashford, Kent, 1902. **Sir Reginald Theodore Blomfield**. b Bow, Devon, 1856. d London, 1942.

Hill Top Beatrix Potter

Lurking behind the onions and carrots of a tousled kitchen garden are the old-fashioned spade, sieve and galvanized watering-can familiar to children around the world reared on *Peter Rabbit* and other tales by Beatrix Potter. Just behind is Hill Top, the working Lakeland farm Potter bought in 1905, where she wrote many of her stories, illustrating

them herself in watercolour, pen and ink. In later years, her compulsion to draw gave way to sheep-breeding (of the native Herdwick sheep) and gardening. No horticultural innovator, she favoured traditional cottage garden plants: azaleas, phlox, roses, saxifrages, hollyhocks, lilies, rock plants and fruit trees, casually interspersed with

vegetables. Her influence endures through her carefully observed illustrations imprinted on the visual memory of each new generation. After her death, she willed more than 1,500 hectares (4,000 acres) of Lake District land along with a number of working farms and cottages to the National Trust.

Hill Top, Sawrey, Hawkshead, Ambleside, Cumbria, 1905. **Beatrix Potter (Helen Beatrix Potter)**. b London, 1866. d Sawrey, Hawkshead, Ambleside, Cumbria, 1943.

Tatton Park Japanese Garden 3rd Baron Egerton

A spectacular autumnal foliage display sets off the thatched teahouse in the Japanese Garden which, created from 1910 by Japanese gardeners brought in for this very purpose, also contained lanterns, stepping-stone bridges, lakes and a Mount Fuji. This addition was in keeping with Tatton's past, which had seen Humphry Repton (in 1791)

and Sir Joseph Paxton (in 1856) add to the garden at the height of their careers. It was the opening up of Japan to the West and the arrival of new and exotic plants in the 1860s that sparked the recurring fad for Japanese gardens. This coincided with the publication of several books describing Japan's gardens, and displays at various

international exhibitions. The natural-looking yet contrived style of Japanese gardens represented a call to abandon the Italianate style or garish bedding schemes in favour of a more natural approach. Other famous Japanese gardens were created at Shipley Glen (1880s), Gunnersbury Park (1900), Fanhams Hall (1901) and Cottered (1905–26).

Tatton Park, Knutsford, Cheshire, 1910. **3rd Baron Egerton**. **b** UK, 1845. **d** UK, 1920.

Folly Farm Sir Edwin Lutyens

Classic elements of the Lutyens style are evident at Folly Farm: formal semicircular steps softened by planting, architectural hedges forming an invitation into the next area of the garden, the Lutyens bench, herringbone brick paving, a red-brick Arts and Crafts house topped by tall chimneys. In partnership with Gertrude Jekyll, Lutyens made some seventy gardens that represent the most satisfactory unification of house and garden in twentieth-century garden design. Lutyens would design a series of formal spaces and vistas enhanced by fine architectural detail, and Jekyll complemented and softened the outlines with sophisticated colour planting. Lutyens was particularly skilled with formal water features: Folly Farm boasts an Indian-inspired pool and canal garden. His most ambitious work is the magnificent, Mughal-inspired Viceroy's Garden in New Delhi.

Folly Farm, Sulhamstead, Reading, Berkshire, 1912. **Sir Edwin Landseer Lutyens**. **b** London, 1869. **d** London, 1944.

"MOONHILL,"
CVCKFIELD, SVSSEX;
For Walter Lloyd Esq:
P. Morley Horder Arcbt.
Thomas H. Mawson. Garden Arcbt.

Moonhill Thomas Mawson

This sketch from Thomas Mawson's book *The Art and Craft of Garden Making* illustrates his approach to design. The house sits above a series of terraces that provide a setting for the beds and borders, all of them well planted, for Mawson was initially a nurseryman, and a collection of ornaments and topiary. The most Edwardian of features,

the rectangular lily pool, graces the lowest level of this area of the garden, which is enclosed by a yew hedge. Although Mawson espoused the Arts and Crafts ideals, he was a formalist and his designs were also influenced by medieval and Renaissance gardens, and by the work of Humphry Repton and Edward Kemp. Mawson was a prolific garden

designer, as well as producing town planning schemes and park designs in Canada, Greece and Australia. He was elected the first president of the Institute of Landscape Architects in 1929. Perhaps the most famous surviving Mawson garden is The Hill in Hampstead, created for Lord Leverhulme, which features a monumental pergola.

Moonhill, Cuckfield, Sussex, 1920s, as depicted in *The Art and Craft of Garden Making*, Thomas Mawson, 1900–26. **Thomas Hayton Mawson**. b Scorton, Lancashire, 1861. d Hest Bank, Lancaster, Lancashire, 1933.

Port Lympne Philip Armstrong Tilden

The Great Stair, constructed from Cumberland stone, rises in 125 steps from the water garden to the parkland above. Despite austerities following World War I, Sir Philip Sassoon commissioned Philip Armstrong Tilden to design Port Lympne as a holiday home — he was in residence only during August — between 1918 and 1921. Described as 'a triumph of beautiful bad taste and Babylonian luxury', the garden comprised a series of terraces and a collection of garden compartments that was almost Victorian in its diversity, including a Striped Garden, Chess Garden, Mogul Court and Pool Lawn. However, it is the nearest England has to an Italian villa garden in purely aesthetic, rather than spiritual terms, and helps demonstrate just how influential the Italian Renaissance garden was between 1900 and 1939. Tilden, who could turn his hand to most styles, became a society architect and garden designer in the 1920s working for, among others, Winston Churchill, David Lloyd George and Lady Warwick.

Port Lympne Gardens, Port Lympne Wild Animal Park, Lympne, Hythe, Kent, 1918–21. **Philip Armstrong Tilden**. b Birmingham, 1887. d Shute, Axminster, Devon, 1956.

Savill Garden Sir Eric Savill

Heathers, rhododendrons, azaleas, camellias and other acid-loving plants thrive at the 14-hectare (35-acre) Savill Garden, a plantsman's garden that also works as an informal landscape designed to show off the plants in a natural way. Eric Savill was deputy surveyor of Windsor Great Park when, in 1932, he began to make a colourful woodland garden under the canopy of fine old oaks, beeches and pines. Today the Savill Garden is one of the best woodland gardens anywhere, with a vast range of species, including a large number of bog plants (ferns, primulas, lysichitons) by the stream that runs through the garden, and a famed narcissus display. The fine dry garden was the first of its kind to be made on this scale in the UK. The adjacent Valley Garden, begun by Savill in 1947, covers a much larger area, and has as its showpiece an azalea display, as well as notable collections of magnolias and rhododendrons.

The Savill Garden, Windsor Great Park, Windsor, Berkshire, 1932. Sir Eric Humphrey Savill. b London, 1895. d Windsor, Berkshire, 1980.

East Lambrook Manor Margery Fish

Although this ebullient display of country cottage flowers — the perfect foil to the manor house — appears old-fashioned, it was actually created from 1938 onwards, over the course of two decades. Margery Fish's particular passion was country cottage herbaceous perennials, which she used to great effect, creating a planting style that was informal, simple and sensible, while keeping her beds filled with a great diversity of interesting plants, both common and unusual. Her approach epitomized the ideal post-war country cottage garden, an idyll attainable by weekend gardeners. Through her writings she helped make perennials fashionable once again, and inspired many other weekend gardeners to follow her naturalistic use of them. She was also instrumental in popularizing the concept of using carpets of weed-smothering species — ground cover — as a form of labour-saving gardening, and was never averse to leaving a weed in situ if it added to the overall planting scheme.

East Lambrook Manor Gardens, South Petherton, Somerset, 1938–69. **Margery Fish. b** 1892. **d** 1969.

Bentley Wood Christopher Tunnard

This garden at Halland in East Sussex was one of a small handful of commissions that Christopher Tunnard, the torch-bearer for the Modernist garden in Britain, received in the 1930s. In his 1938 manifesto, *Gardens in the Modern Landscape*, he railed at informal gardens of herbaceous colour: 'The present-day garden, with the sixpenny novelette, is a last stronghold of romanticism.' Halland featured a large paved terrace all round the Modernist house by Serge Chermayeff, which is on the south side, boldly extended via a straight, narrow path that leads to another terrace with a rectangular grid framing the landscape. It was here, on the platform to the right of the steps, that Tunnard envisaged the placement of a sculpture by Henry Moore. Indeed, Moore's *Recumbent Figure* was briefly installed. Tunnard's example was largely ignored in practical terms, and in the 1940s he moved to the United States to teach at Harvard and Yale, where he continued to publish work on the Modern movement.

Bentley Wood, Halland, Lewes, East Sussex, c1938. **Christopher Tunnard**. b Victoria, British Columbia, Canada, 1910. d United States, 1979.

Sissinghurst Castle Garden Vita Sackville-West

White roses, clematis and honeysuckle combine to create a striking white colour-scheme, which is harmoniously balanced by a background of green. The White Garden at Sissinghurst, Kent, is one of the most influential, small plots of land in recent garden history and started a cult in gardening taste that can still be discerned in gardens from Cape Town to Sydney. Planted in 1948, some eighteen years after Vita Sackville-West and her diplomat husband Harold Nicolson first arrived at the derelict Jacobean estate, the White Garden is just part of the overall layout; a series of 'garden rooms' — formal in shape but informally planted — which first opened to the public in 1938. This was another influential concept, although not one pioneered at this garden. Sackville-West had an enormous influence on gardening taste in the second half of the twentieth century, principally through Sissinghurst and her gardening column in the *Observer* newspaper from 1946 to 1961.

Sissinghurst Castle Garden, Sissinghurst, Cranbrook, Kent, c1930–48. **Vita (Victoria) Sackville-West**. b Knole, Sevenoaks, Kent, 1892. d Sissinghurst, Cranbrook, Kent, 1962.

Dartington Hall Percy Cane

In the Tiltyard at Dartington Hall in Devon, terraced grass banks, a broad York stone stairway and clipped yew hedges combine in a poetic interplay of geometric forms, sharply defined by sunlight and shadow, and contrasting dramatically with the surrounding trees. It is one of the world's most distinctive garden landscapes, located in one of Britain's most magical gardens. Grandeur — as seen in the Tiltyard — is combined with the intimacy of quiet woodland walks, a secluded meadow and a rustic gardener's cottage. Dating back to the fourteenth century, Dartington Hall was built for Richard II's half-brother John Holand. The present garden is largely the work of Percy Cane, a prolific designer whose clients included Haile Selassie. Cane was commissioned by Dorothy and Leonard Elmhirst, who acquired the estate in 1925 and founded the experimental College of Arts. He followed two other consultants used by the Elmhirsts — the American Beatrix Farrand and Harry Avray Tipping.

Dartington Hall, Totnes, Devon, from 1945. **Percy (Stephen Percival) Cane**. b Braintree, Essex, 1881. d Wallingford, Oxfordshire, 1976.

Hidcote Manor Lawrence Johnston

The twin pavilions are set on either side of a grassy path bordered by pleached hornbeams at Hidcote, a hugely influential English garden created by an American, Lawrence Johnston. Johnston inherited the manor and its garden from his mother, and began work in 1907. By the 1920s the garden was well under way. The strong design is defined by high hedges of yew, holly and beech, which act as the walls of a variety of different garden rooms. All the rooms are off to one side of this main vista, which ascends towards the two pavilions. The confident handling of space and scale within these enclosures, and the sophistication and originality of the planting — as here in the red border — have made Hidcote one of the most influential gardens of the twentieth century, often mentioned with Vita Sackville-West's celebrated garden at Sissinghurst. Surprise vistas are a strong feature at Hidcote, and there is a superb bog garden. The garden was bequeathed to the National Trust when Johnston retired to France in 1948.

Hidcote Manor Garden, Hidcote Bartrim, Chipping Campden, Gloucestershire, 1907–48. **Lawrence Waterbury Johnston**. b Paris, France, 1871. d Menton, France, 1958.

Great Dixter Christopher Lloyd

Christopher Lloyd was renowned for the iconoclastic planting experiments in his own garden. He lived at Great Dixter all his life. His father, Nathaniel Lloyd, had laid out the garden's simple framework of yew hedges to complement the Lutyens-designed house. Lloyd retained this rigid structure, but from the 1950s onwards relied on plants alone for effect. He is unsurpassed as an imaginative and artistic plantsman. His articles, lectures and books (notably *The Well-Tempered Garden*, 1970) made him one of the world's best-known gardeners, and innovations at Great Dixter — such as the exotic garden, which replaced a formal rose garden — have been influential. More than any other contemporary gardener, Lloyd demonstrated that plantsmanship at its highest level is an art form that stands comparison with any other. Lloyd's ever-changing combinations of form, colour and texture have made Great Dixter one of the most notable gardens of the late twentieth century.

Great Dixter House & Gardens, Northiam, Rye, East Sussex, from 1950s. **Christopher Lloyd**. b Great Dixter, Northiam, Rye, East Sussex, 1921. d Hastings, East Sussex, 2006.

Barnsley House Rosemary Verey

A modern knot garden of interwoven box hedges (1975) is a delightful feature of the grounds at Barnsley House, the Cotswolds home of Rosemary Verey, leading exponent of the classic English Arts and Crafts country garden in the last decades of the twentieth century. In its 1.6 hectares (4 acres), this immaculate garden epitomizes the style — with exuberant mixed borders, a formal potager, a small Classical temple, shrubby wilderness, laburnum tunnel, yew topiary and well-judged, unostentatious vistas. The house, dating from 1697, stands in the middle. Verey lectured all over the world and her books have been widely translated. Even in post-colonial times, 'English' gardens have continued to be made in all corners of the globe, regardless of climate, native flora or local vernacular. Verey also advised HRH the Prince of Wales on the design of part of his garden at Highgrove, which is quite close to Barnsley House.

Barnsley House, Barnsley, Cirencester, Gloucestershire, from 1951. **Rosemary Verey**. b Gillingham, Kent, 1918. d Cheltenham, Gloucestershire, 2001.

The Gibberd Garden Sir Frederick Gibberd

In this twentieth-century garden of surprises, massive columns in Portland stone and marshalled Coade-stone urns rise from a wild planting of acanthus. Improbably, the statuary came from Coutts Bank in London's Strand, incorporated by the master-planner of Harlow New Town into his eclectic sculpture garden. Gibberd moved here in 1956, inheriting a soaring avenue of limes, a gazebo and a formal pool. Over the years he developed a series of interlocking walled spaces near the house and intimate garden enclosures for his growing collection of sculptures, most of which were modern, as well as play features for his grandchildren. 'I consulted the genius of the place,' he said, 'and then exercised some intuition, without which no art exists.' Within an essentially informal English garden of 2.8 hectares (7 acres), Gibberd introduced an architect's masterly manipulation of space, adding drama to each of his sculptures. After several years of quiet neglect, the garden has been restored by the Gibberd Garden Trust.

The Gibberd Garden, Harlow, Essex, from 1956. **Sir Frederick Ernest Gibberd**. b Coventry, West Midlands, 1908. d Harlow, Essex, 1984.

Templemere Ivor Cunningham & Preben Jakobsen

Templemere is a typical Span development of 65 houses set in 5 hectares (12.5 acres) of artfully designed grounds with a lake surrounded by woodland. Established in 1948, with Eric Lyons as consultant architect, Span's mission was to span 'the gap between the suburban monotony of the typical speculative development and the architecturally designed, individually built residence that has become … financially unattainable'. These affordable houses are designed along Modernist principles with full awareness of how people live. Crucial to the concept was landscape architect Ivor Cunningham. He joined the team in 1955 and worked with Lyons to set the houses in harmony with the site (for example, retaining as many trees as possible) and to conceive designs that united private and public space: the houses defining the setting, and the setting enhancing the houses. Preben Jakobsen, who joined Span in 1961, contributed detailed planting to Cunningham's layouts. The results have been acclaimed by critics ever since.

Templemere Estate and Garden, Weybridge, Surrey, 1963. **Ivor Cunningham**. **b** Orpington, Kent, 1928. **d** Orpington, Kent, 2007. **Preben Jakobsen**. **b** Denmark, 1934.

Turn End Peter Aldington

At Turn End, the house that he designed for his own use, Peter Aldington realized a happy transition from house to garden via an enclosed courtyard, which also encloses a pool and gnarled *Robinia pseudoacacia*. The fact that the three houses and their gardens at the Turn End development were designed as a piece by the same architect, and that this was considered revolutionary even in the 1960s, is symptomatic of the classic division between the landscape and architectural professions. Aldington is an accomplished and imaginative gardener as well as a Modernist architect. The half-acre grounds are packed with incident and feature several separate areas, including a daisy garden and a formal box courtyard planted each year with different brightly coloured annuals. A variety of mature shrubs and trees provides a setting for sculptures. A gravelled area called No-Mans is intensively gardened, with herbaceous perennials, grasses, troughs of alpines and pans of houseleeks.

Turn End, Haddenham, Aylesbury, Buckinghamshire, 1964. **Peter Aldington. b** Preston, Lancashire, 1933.

Wexham Springs Dame Sylvia Crowe

The concrete blocks used for this textured wall contrast with the smooth-cast concrete floor, steps and sculptural water basin, the whole blending with the more natural materials of water-washed cobbles and plant matter. Dame Sylvia Crowe, a contemporary of Sir Geoffrey Jellicoe and Brenda Colvin, was mainly occupied by large-scale commissions such as the layout of new towns, nuclear power stations, forestry plantations, reservoirs and the routing of the National Grid. Her landscape designs reflected loyalty to Capability Brown and Humphry Repton, yet she never lost the connection between the garden and its role, as she observed in *Garden Design*, her magnum opus of 1958: 'Men in every age have felt the need to reconcile themselves with their surroundings, and have created gardens to satisfy their ideals and inspirations.' This ethos is evident in all her gardens. This garden (since demolished) was modern in style, created for the Cement and Concrete Association, and a new-town setting.

Wexham Springs, Wexham, Slough, Buckinghamshire, 1969. **Dame Sylvia Crowe**. b Banbury, Oxfordshire, 1901. d London, 1997.

Ashton Wold Dame Miriam Rothschild

Miriam Rothschild planted clematis, wisteria, ivy, brambles and roses to cover her house. They were allowed to grow as they wish, almost obliterating windows and doors. The Rothschild family lived at Ashton Wold for just over a hundred years. In the 1970s Miriam started to create a wild-flower meadow around the house, sweeping away the original herbaceous borders. The seeds for the meadows were collected from abandoned, undisturbed airfields nearby. Subsequently, Rothschild invented the popular seed mix called Farmer's Nightmare. It consists of corn daisy, feverfew, cornflower, corn marigold, corn cockle and two species of poppy. At the right time of year the meadow, which covers almost 60 hectares (150 acres), looks entirely natural, but to create such a look needs a great deal of energy and much care, so that the individual wild flowers are allowed to bloom and seed profusely.

Ashton Wold, Ashton, Peterborough, Northamptonshire, 1970s. **Dame Miriam Rothschild**. b Ashton Wold, Ashton, Peterborough, Northamptonshire, 1908. d Ashton Wold, Ashton, Peterborough, Northamptonshire, 2005.

Mottisfont Abbey Garden Graham Stuart Thomas

Entering the brick-walled garden, the senses are assailed by the heady colours and fragrances of over 300 varieties of roses and magnificent herbaceous borders. Here, in the fertile soil of the old kitchen garden, Graham Stuart Thomas housed his unique collection of historic shrub roses, now the National Collection of Old-fashioned Roses, many acquired from the Empress Joséphine's late eighteenth-century garden at Malmaison. The garden's tranquillity is heightened by the sound of a splashing fountain and ancient trees, oaks, sweet chestnuts and cedars, recalling days when monks walked the lawns. The garden, created in 1972, comprises four symmetrical lawns surrounded by spacious beds, spilling on to two intercepting main paths or contained by box hedges, entwined with gallica and moss roses. Earlier interesting features at Mottisfont include a Victorian-style bower and Geoffrey Jellicoe's pleached lime alley. Thomas was for many years the National Trust's highly influential gardens adviser.

The Laskett Sir Roy Strong & Dr Julia Trevelyan Oman

A gold-antlered stag is one of many surprises in the intensely personal, autobiographical garden of Sir Roy Strong and his late wife, the theatre designer Dr Julia Trevelyan Oman. The 1.8-hectare (4.5-acre) garden is a series of thirty-two rooms, corridors and ante-chambers, contained by high yew, leylandii and beech hedges that effectively cut out the rest of the world. The garden has been built up gradually, section by section, since the 1970s. Punctuating it are monuments commemorating aspects of the couple's life — a temple is a reminder of Strong's directorship of the Victoria & Albert Museum, for example. A knot garden is testament to Strong's pioneering work in garden history and championing of formality in small spaces during the 1980s. The biographical elements enhance rather than compromise the garden's design strengths, which are the evocation of atmosphere and the manipulation of perspective. The garden is further enriched by an organic kitchen garden.

The Laskett, Much Birch, Hereford, Herefordshire, from 1974. **Sir Roy Strong**. b London, 1935. **Dr Julia Trevelyan Oman**. b London, 1930. d The Laskett, Much Birch, Hereford, Herefordshire, 2003.

Barbara Hepworth Sculpture Garden Dame Barbara Hepworth

Positioned exactly how and where she wanted it, and taking full advantage of changing shadows and surrounding planting, this sculpture is one of a collection of Hepworth's works that transforms the small garden adjacent to her Trewyn Studio into an outside gallery. Studying the sculptures in the way that Hepworth wished them to be seen provides an extra insight into the works themselves and the philosophy behind her art. Hepworth was convinced that 'Full sculptural expression is spatial — it is a three-dimensional realization of the idea, either by mass or spatial construction … There must be a perfect unity between the idea, the substance, and the dimension … The idea … actually is the giving of life and vitality to material … Vitality is not a physical, organic attribute … it is spiritual inner life.' This can be seen in the sculptures themselves, but since it is an ethos that applies equally to garden design, the overall experience is greater than the sum of the individual parts.

Barbara Hepworth Museum & Sculpture Garden, St Ives, Cornwall, c1949–75. **Dame Barbara Hepworth**. b Wakefield, Yorkshire, 1903. d St Ives, Cornwall, 1975.   81

Hatfield House Marchioness of Salisbury

Avenues of evergreen oaks grown on 2-metre (6.4-feet) stems and clipped like lollipops comprise the edges of the East Garden at Hatfield House. The formal beds are box-edged squares, each with a taller box topiary in the middle. The plantings are mixed and random: it is the formal design that holds the garden together. Hatfield House was built for Robert Cecil in 1607. The planting of the original garden was supervised by John Tradescant the Elder. Hatfield now has the most ambitious neo-Jacobean gardens ever made. So successful have Lady Salisbury's designs proved that it comes as a surprise to learn that she did not start work on the East Garden until 1977. Lady Salisbury has written:

'I have tried in the last years to re-make the gardens as they might have been, and bring them back into sympathy with the great unchanging house. It is my dream that one day they will become again a place of fancies and conceits, where not only pleasure and peace can be found but a measure of surprise and mystery.'

Hatfield House, Hatfield, Hertfordshire, from 1977. **Marjorie Gascoyne-Cecil, Marchioness of Salisbury**. b 1922.

Denmans John Brookes

Denmans is the home of garden designer John Brookes, whose book *Room Outside* (1969) popularized the now-familiar concept of outdoor living and 'patio gardening'. The 14-hectare (3.5-acre) garden lies on stony, alkaline soil close to England's south coast. It was begun by the late Joyce Robinson, who arrived in 1946 and subsequently laid out a 'dry river' of gravel, running in sinuous curves down a gentle slope, planted with silver birch trees and Mediterranean-type plants. Robinson's innovative gravel garden was inspired by a visit she had made to the Greek island of Delos in the late 1960s. When Brookes arrived in 1980 he continued the theme of planting in a stony landscape and also made a fragrant, informal herb garden within the former walled kitchen garden. Now in its maturity, this garden shows a relaxed style, at ease with itself, since its most attractive plants are allowed to self-sow, with pleasing informality.

The Grove David Hicks

In the centre of the garden around David Hicks's house is this large reflecting pool surrounded by a stone coping. It is enclosed by a wall of clipped chestnuts, which open out to a chestnut avenue leading to the open landscape beyond. In the distance, approximately a quarter of a mile away, is an obelisk placed as an eyecatcher. Its complete

enclosure by hedges means that visitors remain unaware of the pool, the climax of the design, until they are drawn along the path to its edge. There are few flowers in the garden, as Hicks allowed only pots of annuals on either side of the front door. As a garden created in less than ten years, it is a remarkable achievement by a formalist

designer who understood the relationship between space, scale and surprise. Hicks developed a highly successful international interior design practice, also creating elegant garden designs that reflected the formal English tradition.

The Grove, Brightwell Baldwin, Watlington, Oxfordshire, from 1980s. **David Nightingale Hicks**. b Little Coggeshall, Essex, 1929. d The Grove, Brightwell Baldwin, Watlington, Oxfordshire, 1998.

East Ruston Old Vicarage Graham Robeson & Alan Gray

The sunken garden at the Old Vicarage is part of a recently built Arts and Crafts garden worthy of Lutyens and the Edwardian era. The owners began their garden in the 1980s and have energetically expanded it ever since. It is a typical English mix of formal architecture softened by luxuriant and imaginative planting: the brick walls, garden buildings and gates are of the highest quality, but they are nevertheless upstaged by the planting. As well as classic herbaceous borders (enlivened by grasses), box parterres and high yew hedges, the garden is packed with rare and tender plants, and boasts a Mediterranean garden and a tropical border influenced by Christopher Lloyd. High yew hedges afford an effective shelter from strong winds off the North Sea, which is only 3.2 kilometres (2 miles) away. Gaps in the yew frame vistas over fields towards two church towers, which serve as dynamic eyecatchers. The energy of the owners means the Old Vicarage is set to become a twenty-first-century Sissinghurst or Hidcote.

East Ruston Old Vicarage, East Ruston, Norwich, Norfolk, from 1980s. **Graham Robeson**. Active UK, late twentieth and early twenty-first centuries.
Alan Gray. Active UK, late twentieth and early twenty-first centuries.

Little Peacocks Brenda Colvin

Little Peacocks was Brenda Colvin's private garden. The planting is naturalistic but diverse, and the range of spring flowers and foliage creates a perfect foil to the lovely Cotswold house. As the seasons change, so does the display, and the selection of species and their arrangement amply demonstrates Colvin's wide plant knowledge and

planting design skills. Such talents were also put to use in other, larger-scale garden schemes, notably the Riverside Garden at Buscot Park and the replanting of the Manor House garden in Sutton Courtenay. Colvin was a founder member of the Landscape Institute (formed in 1929 as the British Association of Garden Architects) and author of

one of the first standard texts of the new profession — *Land and Landscape* (1947). In her professional capacity as a landscape architect, she was responsible for several urban design commissions. Among them was the military town of Aldershot, Hampshire, as well as power stations, land reclamation projects and reservoirs.

Little Peacocks, Filkins, Lechlade, Gloucestershire, 1955–81. **Brenda Colvin**. **b** Simla, India, 1897. **d** Little Peacocks, Filkins, Lechlade, Gloucestershire, 1981.

Sutton Place Sir Geoffrey Jellicoe

A much-enlarged version of a relief sculpture by Ben Nicholson, surrounded by yew hedges and prefaced by a rectangular pond, is the endpiece of Geoffrey Jellicoe's major (albeit unfinished) work, the garden at Sutton Place commissioned by Stanley Seeger in 1980. Jellicoe's intention was to make a Modernist garden of distinct features that were intended to be visited in a specific order. The programme is based on man's passage through life, from birth to death, and is informed by Jellicoe's preoccupation with the philosophy of Carl Jung. Birth is represented by a huge lake in the shape of a foetus; death and beyond by the Nicholson wall. Surviving features at Sutton Place include a Surrealist walk — a homage to Magritte, with huge urns that create an optical illusion — and the Paradise Garden, a delightful space of meandering paths, fountains and rose arbours. Jellicoe was an architect who turned to landscape after a tour of Italian Renaissance gardens in the 1920s.

Sutton Place, Sutton Park, Sutton Green, Guildford, Surrey, 1980–6. **Sir Geoffrey Jellicoe**. b London, 1900. d Seaton, Devon, 1996.

The Lost Gardens of Heligan Tim Smit

Fallen tree trunks evoke a sense of prehistory in the Jungle Garden, a lush subtropical landscape of giant bamboos, primeval tree ferns and mysterious pools. Heligan, in Cornwall, is a time-capsule garden. Laid out during the eighteenth and nineteenth centuries by the Tremayne family, it was neglected for much of the last century. Then, in 1990, archaeologist-turned-record-producer Tim Smit cut through the 5-metre (15-feet) high brambles with a machete and began uncovering a garden that had lain unchanged for almost a hundred years. Smit and his team have turned Heligan into one of the most visited private gardens in Britain, partly by shrewd marketing and partly by cleverly preserving something of the garden's feeling of being 'lost'. The 32-hectare (80-acre) site includes a vertiginous ravine, a charming Italian Garden, a grotto and some magnificent rhododendrons. The working areas include a walled vegetable garden with a pineapple pit heated by manure.

The Lost Gardens of Heligan, Pentewan, St Austell, Cornwall, begun 1990. **Tim Smit. b** Scheveningen, The Hague, The Netherlands, 1954.

Private Garden Arabella Lennox-Boyd

This elegant little garden of clipped box is part of the private garden at Ascott, where Arabella Lennox-Boyd has created a formal design filled with subtly original ideas. Lennox-Boyd's confidence with such formal schemes, and her ability to lift them above mere historical pastiche, is perhaps partly due to her Italian background. The relatively substantial clipped hedges, with low domes within, echo the shape and scale of the central water feature to create a vision of effortless felicity. Elsewhere in the garden Lennox-Boyd demonstrates her skill as a plantswoman in the English mode, although her style is always distinguished by an underlying formal rigour. One of the most effective innovations at Ascott is her use of an uncompromising black as the decorative colour for the built features. Offset by planting, it does not look remotely funereal. In the 1980s and 1990s Lennox-Boyd established herself as Britain's prime society garden designer.

Private Garden, Ascott, Wing, Leighton Buzzard, Buckinghamshire, c1990. **Arabella Lennox-Boyd**. Active UK, late twentieth and early twenty-first centuries.

Fulham Garden Anthony Noel

This view seems to draw the visitor out of the house and into Anthony Noel's own London town garden. Romantic white lilies and petunias in pots contrast with the formality of clipped box, and variegated ivy 'papers' the wall. Ex-actor Noel combines a penchant for theatricality and glamour with a sure handling of space, particularly on a small scale. His original ideas, such as a beach-hut shed or rows of jauntily striped, painted terracotta pots planted with tiny lollipop box trees, have been copied many times over in recent years. Noel's spatial confidence means he uses large-scale urns, plants or trellised supports in a small space, but always with the same sure elegance. His gardens are carefully lit because his urban, London clientele use their gardens as much at night as in the day. Noel's work is unusual in that it has been focused almost exclusively on the small-scale.

Fulham Garden, London, 1990s. **Anthony Noel**. Active UK, late twentieth and early twenty-first centuries.

Gravel Garden Beth Chatto

It is still possible to create a spectacular display of plants, even when the growing medium is nothing but 60 cm (2 ft) of gravel and sand overlaying clay. The Gravel Garden, which was once the car park for Beth Chatto's garden, was made in 1991. Its inspiration was a dried-up river bed in New Zealand, where a wide range of plants thrived on the inhospitable banks. The garden is an extension of the concept of working with nature. By taking the decision never to water or feed the garden, to let the plants live or die on their own ability to withstand her conditions, Chatto experienced the sad deaths of unsuitable plants and the joy when others thrived. But 'survival of the fittest' is only half of the experiment. The other half has been the careful crafting of the plant associations in order to create a display of flowers, form and foliage that looks stunning all year round and remains relatively low-maintenance.

Gravel Garden (The Beth Chatto Gardens), Elmstead Market, Colchester, Essex, 1991. **Beth Chatto. b** UK, 1923.

The Garden in Mind Ivan Hicks

A spring coiled around a head of David began a series of echoing spiral shapes flanked by ghostly floating ornaments. Further back, paulownia trees formed into hands grasp rusting antique gardening tools. When you entered The Garden in Mind — a walled, former kitchen garden at Stansted Park — reality dissolved. Its designer,

Ivan Hicks, worked for ten years as head gardener to Edward James, the eccentric patron of Surrealist artists Dalí and Magritte. Blending this formative experience with fragments from myth and literature, Hicks made a garden that was dreamlike in the most literal sense — seemingly irrational, it was full of hidden meanings. Within a layout

based on the ancient metaphor of the World Tree, he designed symbolic rooms, paths and mounds, and surreal installations. Plants were trimmed, shaped or fused to make living artworks and arches. Since the late 1990s, Hicks has been working on The Enchanted Forest at Groombridge Place, Sussex.

The Garden in Mind, Stansted Park, Rowland's Castle, Hampshire, 1991 (since demolished). **Ivan Hicks**. b Donnington Castle, Derbyshire, 1944.

Golders Green Garden Paul Cooper

A projection of Roy Lichtenstein's iconic Pop Art piece *Wham!* enlivens the night-time ambience of a small north London garden. The garden's owners intended to use the garden mainly at night, so Paul Cooper incorporated smooth white panels into his design to provide the potential for constantly changing visuals in this enclosed space.

Architectural and textile designs are particularly effective projections. Metal balustrades section off small areas of the decked terrace, and a selection of shrubs grown for their foliage effects (hebes, bamboos, euphorbias) are confined to raised planters. A stainless-steel cascade — cleverly lit — adds to the nocturnal drama. Cooper is an

iconoclastic figure in contemporary garden design, well known for showcasing outrageous ideas, such as floating planters or mid-air hanging baskets, at Chelsea Flower Show. On one occasion he was censured for incorporating erotic drawings in his design.

Golders Green Garden, London, 1992, renovated 2001. **Paul Cooper**. b Manchester, 1949.

Prospect Cottage Derek Jarman

Derek Jarman's unique, totemic sculptures, made of pebbles and flotsam, and his exuberant and unlikely plantings, surround a small, wooden, fisherman's cottage on an exposed pebble beach in Kent, in the shadow of the Dungeness B nuclear power station. The garden rapidly became (and still is) a cult destination, inspiring many imitations, most of them poor. 'I invest my stones with the power of Avebury,' Jarman wrote. 'I have read all the mystical books about leylines and circles — I built the circles with this behind my mind.' In the unearthly and beautiful landscape of Dungeness, Jarman's sculptures of driftwood, rusted metal and weathered stones took on a magical quality. The success of his gardening was equally arresting, with bright poppies, marigolds, irises and dog roses thriving next to the less surprising sea kale, santolina and cotton lavender. The garden survives.

Heveningham Hall Kim Wilkie

Turf terraces create an informal green amphitheatre behind Heveningham Hall mansion, where the estate was landscaped by Capability Brown in the eighteenth century. Kim Wilkie was allocated the task of accurately restoring the large-scale Brownian landscape, but he was given a free rein when it came to the formal Victorian garden which lay behind the house, the site of which is shown here. Wilkie's new scheme contains sympathetic echoes of eighteenth-century precedents — such as the turf amphitheatre by Charles Bridgeman at Claremont — but it is nevertheless unmistakably contemporary. Wilkie specializes in fusing modern design and practical needs with historic landscapes. These aims are shown in other projects, which include the long-term regeneration plan for the Thames Landscape Strategy and the redesign of the outdoor spaces in Beirut's old port area.

Heveningham Hall, Heveningham, Halesworth, Suffolk, from 1995. **Kim Wilkie**. **b** UK, 1955.

The Latin Garden Christopher Bradley-Hole

This 'Virgilian' garden comprised sleek rendered walls, stainless steel, glass panels, contemporary furniture and a bold axis along the whole length of the plot. Quotations from the *Eclogues* were inscribed on stone plaques, a device borrowed from Ian Hamilton Finlay's Little Sparta. London's annual Chelsea Flower Show is not known as a fount of design innovation, but in 1997 Christopher Bradley-Hole's winning show garden, sponsored by the *Daily Telegraph*, marked a stylistic turning point — away from the pastiche of Arts and Crafts, which had reigned supreme for decades. Bradley-Hole is an uncompromising Modernist. The planting utilized a pared-down but effective palette of striking specimens: tall irises and drumstick alliums provided dramatic purple notes above an underplanting of grasses. His example led to a vogue for Classical-contemporary show gardens at Chelsea, although the judging panel's need for horticultural sophistication still militates against many contemporary design approaches.

The Latin Garden, Chelsea Flower Show, London, 1997. **Christopher Bradley-Hole**. b Sussex, 1955.

Pensthorpe Piet Oudolf

Trained as an architect, Oudolf, a Dutch horticulturist and plantsman, is the leading proponent of the 'New Perennial Movement'. Inspired by nature, art and time, he is renowned for planting meadows composed of drifts of perennials and ornamental grasses — an approach he uses to great effect on large-scale public projects, such as this 0.4-hectare (1-acre) Millennium Garden at Pensthorpe. Oudolf's trademark is his use of bold, contrasting arrangements that rely on the plants' colour, form, texture and scent for impact, an effect enhanced by the play of light and movement. In addition to their beauty, his gardens are practical and resilient (right plant, right place) and offer seasonal interest. His work is an extension of the perennial meadows pioneered in 1930s Germany by Karl Foerster, and developed in the 1970s by Wolfgang Oehme and James van Sweden as the New American Garden — 'the simple beauty and grandeur of the American prairie defined by large sweeps of herbaceous perennials and grasses'.

Pensthorpe (Pensthorpe Waterfowl Park), Pensthorpe, Fakenham, Norfolk, 2000. **Piet Oudolf**. b Haarlem, The Netherlands, 1944.

Home Farm Dan Pearson

With training and experience at the RHS's Wisley and the Royal Botanic Gardens at Kew and Edinburgh, together with extensive studying of native wild flower communities in Europe and the Himalayas, Dan Pearson has a deep understanding of plants and nature. His design approach combines this ethos of plants' needs with an empathetic

appreciation of the natural environment, a plantsman's artistic eye and a sympathetic treatment of the genius of place. In the case of Home Farm, this included product consultant Frances Mossman, the owner, who worked in close partnership with Pearson for over a decade. Work began in 1987, when Home Farm was just a derelict

building and an overgrown wilderness. The garden, which covers 1.6 ha (4 acres), now boasts a Woodland Garden, a Lime Enclosure, a Thyme Lawn, a Vegetable Garden — all of which epitomize Pearson's naturalistic, untamed style. Another of Pearson's trademarks is a seamless transition between the indoor and outdoor environments.

Home Farm, Northamptonshire, 1987–2001. Dan Pearson. b UK, 1964.

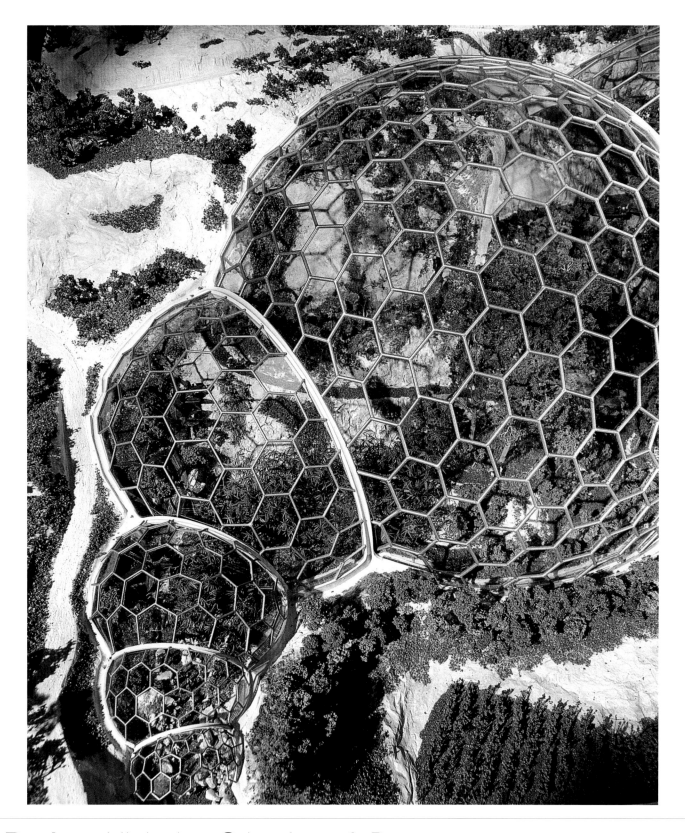

Eden Project Nicholas Grimshaw & Partners

These biomes are the focal point of a visitor attraction and educational project built in a disused china clay pit in Cornwall. The 14-hectare (34.5-acre) bowl-shaped site is 60 metres (192 feet) deep with steep, south-facing walls that catch the sun. The biomes are giant conservatories, manufactured with the latest technology and materials and designed to be as energy-efficient as possible. Inside them, two of the world's climate zones have been recreated: the humid tropics (rainforests and Oceania) and the warm temperate regions (the Mediterranean, South African Cape and California). The biomes are alive with plants native to these regions to create a natural and sustainable eco-system. Another, roofless, biome is the temperate zone, and the planting reflects the huge range of native British and exotic plants that thrive in the mild climate of Cornwall.

Eden Project, Bodelva, St Austell, Cornwall, 2001. **Nicholas Grimshaw & Partners**. **Nicholas Grimshaw**. b Hove, East Sussex, 1939.

Cowley Manor Noël Kingsbury

The pink-buff flower spikes of *Macleaya cordata*, crimson globes of *Knautia macedonica* and the arching leaves of the grass *Miscanthus sinensis* 'Silver Feather' are just a few of the plants in the dramatic borders flanking the formal lawn at Cowley Manor. This is the setting for Noël Kingsbury's radical experiment in nature-inspired planting, begun in 1996 when the owners approached him to replant the garden. Further from the house, perennials are massed in great swathes, the result resembling what he describes as 'a cross between a traditional border and a wild-flower meadow'. Unlike conventional schemes, these 'open borders' can be walked around and through, creating constantly changing associations of form and colour, and magical lighting effects. Kingsbury is a leading proponent of this 'New Perennial' planting style. As with the Continental designers who have influenced him, his approach is both ecologically friendly and low in maintenance.

Cowley Manor, Cowley, Cheltenham, Gloucestershire, 1996–2002. **Noël Kingsbury**. b Reading, Berkshire, 1957.

Split Tony Heywood

Educated as an archaeologist and anthropologist, Heywood now describes himself neither as a garden designer nor a sculptor, but a horticultural installation artist. He is known for producing installations ranging in size from the small — for example, 'micro-landscapes' cultivated in a petri dish — to grandiose schemes that cover extensive areas. Site-specific and utilizing unorthodox materials often in allegorical ways, Heywood's works are at the cutting edge of conceptual garden art. Created for the International Festival of the Garden at Westonbirt, Split is typical of his style. Featuring two reflective, modular 'flat pack' monoliths with planting pockets, this unorthodox garden is set within undulating mounds of sward, separated by a valley of stone. In his own words, Heywood's approach is an 'attempt to cross-fertilize the areas of garden design and fine art' using both 'plant and inert matter'. As such his works are 'pure spectacle and ... not functional ... not to be entered and should be seen as contemplative works'.

Split, International Festival of the Garden, Westonbirt, The National Arboretum, Tetbury, Gloucestershire, 2003. **Tony Heywood**. Active UK, twenty-first century.

National Lottery Garden Diarmuid Gavin

Called 'A Colourful Suburban Eden', the most striking feature of this garden, whose design was dominated by curvaceous lines and both circular and oval forms, was the arrangements of painted steel spheres. Inspired by the numbered balls used in the National Lottery draws, the balls were arrayed together in this multi-coloured sinuous

wave sculpture reminiscent of pins stuck into a pincushion. The balls were also used to cover the roof of the oval pavilion or pod, just visible in the distance. While the balls certainly introduced colour, the planting scheme did not. Contrastingly, and perhaps inspired by Gavin's native Emerald Isle, the planting was dominated by a foliage show

of different tints and tones of green, with an emphasis on those species with an architectural form. Gavin's designs are contemporary and ingenious in their use of materials. He studied at the College of Amenity Horticulture at the Botanic Gardens in Glasnevin, Dublin, and as well as designing gardens has presented various television series.

National Lottery Garden, Chelsea Flower Show, London, 2004. **Diarmuid Gavin**. b London, 1964.

Daily Telegraph Garden Tom Stuart-Smith

Following a degree in zoology, Tom Stuart-Smith studied to become a landscape architect, and after a decade or so working on a number of historic garden projects for two of the most respected practices in the UK, he established his own practice in 1998. Now a regular winner at Chelsea, Stuart-Smith described this 'Best in Show' garden as a sort of fusion between romanticism and Modernism, with its contrast of rich colours, strong textures, effuse planting and diversity of natural materials, which are united within a Minimalist, asymmetric plan. Certainly the rich planting scheme is romantic, dominated by a show of deep, saturated colours — blues, purples, violets, whites and the rusty-orange of the irises. The latter unite the living with the inanimate pre-rusted Corten steel walls, water tanks and rill. The path of Herefordshire cobble draws the eye through the garden, while the green bed to its left and the hornbeam hedge provide the perfect foil and contrast to this abundant and vibrant display.

The Daily Telegraph Garden, Chelsea Flower Show, London, 2006. **Tom Stuart-Smith**. **b** 1960. Active UK, late twentieth and early twenty-first centuries.

Glossary

Allée

Straight walk, path or ride bordered by trees or clipped hedges. A series of *allées* often form a geometric pattern (see **patte d'oie**). *See pages 14, 18, 23 and 47*

Alpines *see* Winter garden

Annuals

Plants (usually, in a garden context, brightly coloured flowers) that live for a single year. They germinate from seed in the spring, are then planted out to flower in summer, then set seed and die as winter approaches. Annuals are the plants most often used in formal **carpet-bedding** displays. *See pages 76 and 84*

Arboretum

A **botanic garden** for the display of trees and shrubs — often, rare native species in danger of being lost or star exotic introductions. *See pages 37, 40, 45, 46 and 59*

Arts and Crafts

Late nineteenth-century British movement, promoted by William Morris, John Ruskin and others, that extolled a return to the perceived values of medieval craftsmanship as a reaction to increasing industrialization. In a garden context, Arts and Crafts style often refers specifically to the work of Gertrude Jekyll and Sir Edwin Lutyens and their followers working in the first two decades of the twentieth century. *See pages 49, 53, 57, 63, 64, 73 and 85*

Baroque

Seventeenth- and eighteenth-century European style making exuberant use of ornamentation. In a garden context, Baroque features include richly carved fountains, **nymphaeums**, water tricks, **grottoes** and statuary.

Bosquet

A small clump of trees, or a decorative glade with statuary, enclosed by a hedge or fence, usually a part of a seventeenth- or eighteenth-century French formal landscape.

Botanic garden

A representative collection of plants, from a particular geographic location or specific botanical groups (rare and exotic examples such as orchids, ferns, rhododendrons) for which, especially during the eighteenth and nineteenth centuries, plant hunters gathered new and rare species on expeditions abroad. Increasingly, motivated by scientific reasons rather than perpetuating the private collection as a status symbol of the wealthy. *See pages 16, 24 and 51*

Carpet bedding

Nineteenth-century practice of planting out young seedlings of **annual** plants *en masse* to create abstract effects based on masses of colours. A technique still used widely in municipal parks worldwide.

Chinoiserie

Chinese-style decoration as imagined by European designers from the seventeenth century onwards. It was based mainly on travellers' descriptions — although the architect William Chambers championed the style in the eighteenth century — and was influential throughout Europe. *See page 24*

English landscape style

Garden design style formulated during the first years of the eighteenth century, first as an art form analogous to literature, with complex symbolic and political meanings expressed as buildings and landscape features. Later, it became a purely visual or painterly medium, evocative of a pastoral idyll — as with the work of Capability Brown. A style reproduced throughout Europe in the eighteenth and nineteenth centuries. *See pages 13, 15, 18, 19, 20, 21, 22, 25, 30 and 32*

Exedra

Generally, in Greek and Roman architecture, a building standing apart from the main dwelling, often in the garden. Its main feature is its accessibility to light (of the sun or moon), conducive to quiet contemplation, learned discussion or less formal conversation. *See page 17*

Eyecatcher

Structure in the wider landscape designed to draw the eye and provide a focus in a broad vista. Eyecatchers are usually buildings, often towers, with a romantic aspect. *See pages 29, 32, 84 and 85*

Ferme ornée

Precursor of the **English landscape style**: a working farm ornamented by seats, temples, viewpoints and walks. *Fermes ornées* were generally of modest size and cheap to create. William Shenstone and Philip Southcote created celebrated examples. *See page 19*

Floriculture

The cultivation of flowers or flowering plants, which had a surge of popularity during the nineteenth century. John Claudius Loudon (1783–1843), a prodigious author of reference books on gardening and agriculture, commented in his *Encyclopaedia of Gardening* (1822) that 'Floriculture is obviously of limited interest … compared to horticulture'. *See page 34*

Folly

A built structure whose principal purpose is decorative or whimsical rather than practical; occasionally a utility building made to look like a historic, ruined or fantastical structure. *See page 33*

Gazon coupé

Grass with shapes cut out of turf and filled with coloured earths or gravels. Used principally in England in the seventeenth century for formal **parterre** designs.

Gothic style

More accurately described as Gothic Revival, this movement, led by architecture, belongs chiefly to the late eighteenth and the nineteenth centuries and was a conscious choice in contrast to the accepted current style — that is, Classicism. The style, the main feature of which was the pointed arch, was also adopted by the other arts for its transcendental, romantic qualities. With Horace Walpole's Strawberry Hill, Gothic Revival became the fashion. *See pages 17, 29 and 31*

Grotto

A cave-like room, usually man-made, decorated with shells, minerals and fossils. Italian Renaissance grottoes were semi-open structures set in the open garden. Later, in eighteenth-century England, grottoes began to be made as discrete buildings — sometimes underground — lined with shells and minerals. *See pages 6, 8, 13, 17, 19, 21, 23, 29 and 88*

Ha-ha

A sunken 'fence', resembling a dry ditch or moat with one vertical stone side. It allowed livestock to graze on pasture quite close to the house, furthering the illusion of pastoral ease in eighteenth-century landscape gardens. *See pages 12, 31 and 48*

Herbaceous border

Areas that consist entirely of **perennial** plants that die back to an underground root every winter, then re-grow in spring. In practice, most 'herbaceous' borders are in fact mixed borders: i.e. they also contain evergreens, bulbs and **annuals**. *See pages 41, 52, 53, 57, 67, 69, 76, 79, 85, 97, 98 and 100*

Hermitage

Originally conceived as places of retreat or meditation, hermitages became fashionable in Britain during the eighteenth century. The primitive and rustic structures were designed to house real hermits but often wax or even clockwork models were used instead. *See pages 6, 26 and 29*

Italianate

The Italianate style, which was very influential between 1900 and 1939, was based on Italian Renaissance motifs. Terraced formal gardens, often including water cascades, pools and fountains, were laid out on the Italian model. See, for example, Sir Charles Barry's creation at Harewood House. *See pages 7, 42, 54, 58, 60, 62 and 65*

Knot garden

An enclosed garden, based on **Tudor** precedents, comprising low evergreen hedges, usually box, yew or thyme, planted to create an intricate and pleasing symmetrical pattern, sometimes with infills of brightly coloured flowers or gravel. *See pages 4, 73 and 80*

Landscape style *see* English landscape style

Latin plant names

The two-word plant-naming system was devised by Swedish botanist Linnaeus (hence the Linnean system) in the eighteenth century. The first word is the genus; the second is the species. The system is useful as it is precise, accurate and international. However, it means that plant names can be hard to pronounce and difficult to remember.

Modernism

Style formulated in the 1920s, characterized by architecture that could be mass-produced and the use of modern materials such as concrete. The 'white-cube' building is an archetypal Modernist style. A variety of garden styles have been used in an attempt to complement the building style.
See pages 68, 75, 76, 77, 87, 96 and 103

Native plants

Plants that naturally occur in the wild in a given area. In nineteenth-century horticulture the emphasis was on recently introduced exotic plants, but from the late twentieth century there has been increasing interest in native flora and this has impacted on design.
See pages 52 and 98

New Perennial movement/style

A naturalistic planting style composed of big and bold drifts of hardy **perennials** and ornamental grasses. Most effective on a large scale, it is a concept which has the benefit of being low maintenance.
See pages 97, 98 and 100

Nymphaeum

Semicircular structure, often semi-open, containing statuary on the theme of rustic nymphs and water.

Objet trouvé

From the French for 'found object'. The integration into the garden's design of objects of daily use such as mirrors or crockery and natural shells or stones goes back to the Renaissance and flourished in **Baroque** and **Rococo** gardens. In more recent times, however, it became the hallmark of the fantastic environments created by self-taught eccentrics or 'outsider' artists. Elements can be seen in Derek Jarman's Prospect Cottage and Ivan Hicks's Garden of the Mind.
See pages 92 and 94

Parterre

Formal terrace decorated in one of a variety of styles, from simple patterns of cut turf and gravel (**gazon coupé**) to intricate designs made of hedges, grass, gravel, turf and flowers (*parterre de broderie*).
See pages 8, 9, 10, 11, 12, 51, 54, and 85

Patte d'oie

A number of straight **allées**, vistas, paths or avenues (usually three or five) diverging from a common point, suggesting the shape of a goose's foot (*patte d'oie*).
See page 17

Perennials *see* Herbaceous border

Pergola

Wooden and/or stone structure that forms a covered walkway, often planted with climbers such as roses, vines or wisteria.
See pages 53, 56 and 60

Picturesque

Late eighteenth-century landscape style (almost exclusively English) that celebrates the power of untamed nature, frequently in a setting of extreme terrain. Loosely used to describe the **English landscape style** in Europe. The term comes from the idea of making landscapes in the manner of pictures.
See pages 22, 25, 28, 33, 39 and 48

Pinetum

An **arboretum** specializing in pines and other conifers, for scientific or ornamental purposes.
See page 45

Plantsman, -woman

A particular style of garden where planting and the use of plants is a defining feature or an intrinsic part of its design. Christopher Lloyd's Great Dixter is a prime example of plants used imaginatively and for effect.
See pages 56, 57, 59, 66, 67, 69, 71, 72, 85, 86, 91, 97, 98 and 100

Potager

French-style decorative kitchen garden, edged with box and incorporating vegetables grown partly for their appearance.
See page 73

Rill

With their origins in early Persian gardens, a rill is a narrow, shallow man-made stream or rivulet, usually lined with stone, and used on a gentle gradient to convey water from one area of the garden to another. Rills can be serpentine — a famous example is William Kent's rill at Rousham — or linear, as used by Sir Edwin Lutyens and Gertrude Jekyll in their **Arts and Crafts** gardens.
See pages 20 and 103

Rococo

Exuberant eighteenth-century decorative style derived from *rocaille*, the Italian word for shell. In Rococo gardens, decoration is at least as important as form.
See page 27

Romantic style

Refers to the landscaping style evolved from the **English landscape** movement and corresponding with the European literary and philosophical Romantic movement. Usually involving sweeping lawns, wooded groves, ponds or lakes and follies, it became widespread in Europe throughout the nineteenth century, often at the expense of older formal gardens.
See pages 30, 35, 39, 44 and 103

Serpentine paths

Curving or twisting paths running through areas of shrub and tree planting. Serpentine paths frequently lend a note of informality to otherwise symmetrical schemes.
See pages 14, 17, 23 and 27

Topiary

The art of clipping evergreen plants, such as box and yew, into abstract or figurative shapes.
See pages 11, 12, 53, 54, 58, 64, 73, 82 and 89

Tudor garden

Gardens made in Britain during the Tudor period (1485–1603). **Knot gardens** were a principal motif of the gardens of this type.
See page 4

Wilderness

Enclosed, informal areas in a landscape garden, planted with trees and shrubs and featuring **serpentine** walks.
See pages 8, 47 and 73

Winter garden

Alpine or rock garden, or an indoor heated conservatory for the display of exotic plants.

Directory

Garden opening times vary throughout the year and access may be limited during restoration work. It is advisable to check the dates and times of opening prior to visiting or making travel arrangements. Private gardens are not listed unless they are open to the public.

Berkshire

The Savill Garden 1932
Windsor Great Park, Windsor
Open daily, Mar to Oct, 10am to 6pm;
Nov to Feb, 10am to 4.30pm
www.theroyallandscape.co.uk

Buckinghamshire

Stowe Landscape Gardens 1779
Stowe, Buckingham
Parkland open daily, Mon to Sun,
dawn to dusk
www.nationaltrust.org.uk

Turn End 1964
Townside, Haddenham, Aylesbury
Open occasionally through the
National Gardens Scheme
www.ngs.org.uk

Cheshire

Arley Hall & Gardens 1840s
Arley, Northwich
Open Mar to Sep, Tues to Sun & Bank
Holidays, 11am to 5pm; Oct, Sun,
12pm to 5pm
www.arleyhallandgardens.com

Tatton Park 1910
Knutsford
Gardens open Mar to Sep, Tues to Sun
(and Mon in Aug), 10am to 6pm;
Sep to Mar, Tues to Sun, 11am to 4pm
www.tattonpark.org.uk

Cornwall

**Barbara Hepworth Museum &
Sculpture Garden** 1975
Barnoon Hill, St Ives
Open daily, Mar to Oct, 10am to
5.20pm; open Nov to Feb, Tues to Sun,
10am to 4.20pm (or dusk)
www.tate.org.uk/stives

Caerhays Castle Gardens 1890s
Gorran, St Austell
Gardens open daily, Feb to Jun,
10am to 5pm
www.caerhays.co.uk

Eden Project 2001
Bodelva, St Austell
Open daily, summer, 10am to 6pm;
winter, 10am to 4.30pm
Closed Christmas Eve &
Christmas Day
www.edenproject.com

The Lost Gardens of Heligan 1990
Pentewan, St Austell
Open Mar to Oct, 10am to 6pm;
Nov to Feb, 10am to 5pm
Closed Christmas Eve &
Christmas Day
www.heligan.com

Cumbria

Brantwood 1871
Coniston
Open daily, Mar to Nov, 11am to
5.30pm; Nov to Mar, 11am to 4.30pm
www.brantwood.org.uk

Hill Top 1905
Sawrey, Hawkshead, Ambleside
Garden open daily, Feb, 10am to 4pm;
open Mar, Sat & Sun, 10am to 4pm;
open daily, Mar to Nov, 10.30am to
5pm; open daily, Nov to Dec,
10am to 4pm
www.nationaltrust.org.uk

Levens Hall & Gardens 1712
Kendal
Gardens open Mar to Oct, Sun to
Thurs, 10am to 5pm
www.levenshall.co.uk

Rydal Mount & Gardens 1850
Rydal, Ambleside
Open daily except Tues, Mar to Oct,
9.30am to 5pm; Nov, Dec & Feb,
10am to 4pm
Closed Jan, Christmas Day
& Boxing Day
www.rydalmount.co.uk

Derbyshire

Chatsworth 1858
Bakewell
Garden open daily, 11am to 6pm
www.chatsworth.org

Derby Arboretum 1840
Derby
Open daily, 8am to 6pm
www.derbyarboretum.co.uk

Devon

Dartington Hall 1945
Totnes
Gardens open daily, dawn to dusk;

tours by appointment
(see website for further details)
www.dartingtonhall.com

Dorset

Athelhampton House & Gardens
1890s
Athelhampton, Dorchester
Open Mar to Oct, Sun to Thurs,
10.30am to 5pm; Nov to Feb, Sun,
10.30am to 5pm
www.athelhampton.co.uk

East Sussex

Great Dixter House & Gardens
1950s
Northiam, Rye
Gardens open Mar to Oct, Tues to
Sun & Bank Holiday Mondays, 11am
to 5pm
www.greatdixter.co.uk

The Royal Pavilion 1808
Brighton
Open daily, Apr to Sep, 9.30am to
5.45pm; Oct to Mar, 10am to 5.15pm;
open Christmas Eve, 10am to 2.30pm
Closed Christmas Day & Boxing Day
www.royalpavilion.org.uk

Essex

The Beth Chatto Gardens 1991
Elmstead Market, Colchester
Open Mon to Sat, 9am to 5pm
www.bethchatto.co.uk

The Gibberd Garden 1956
Harlow
Open Apr to Sep, Wed, Sat, Sun
& Bank Holidays, 2pm to 6pm
www.thegibberdgarden.co.uk

Warley Place 1900
Essex Wildlife Trust Reserve,
Great Warley, Brentwood
Open days are by appointment
(see website for further details)
www.warleyplace.org.uk

Gloucestershire

Barnsley House 1951
Barnsley, Cirencester
Now a hotel and spa, gardens open to
hotel guests; also occasionally through
the National Gardens Scheme
(see website for further details)
www.barnsleyhouse.com
www.ngs.org.uk

Cowley Manor 2002
Cowley, Cheltenham
Now a hotel and spa, gardens open
to hotel guests
www.cowleymanor.com

Hidcote Manor Garden 1948
Hidcote Bartrim, Chipping Campden
Open Mar to Jun and Sep, Mon to
Wed, Sat & Sun, 10am to 6pm; Jul
to Aug, Mon to Wed, Fri to Sat, 10am
to 6pm; Oct, Mon to Wed, Sat & Sun,
10am to 5pm
www.nationaltrust.org.uk

Highnam Court Gardens 1849
Highnam, Gloucester
Open through the National Gardens
Scheme, Apr to Sep, 1st Sun in the
month, 11am to 5pm; also open for
other specific events (see website for
further details)
www.highnamcourt.co.uk

Kelmscott Manor 1871
Kelmscott, Lechlade
Open Apr to Sep, Wed, 11am to 5pm;
certain Saturdays (see website for
further details), 2pm to 5pm; gardens
also open, Jun to Sep, Thurs, 2pm
to 5pm
www.kelmscottmanor.co.uk

Little Peacocks 1981
Filkins, Lechlade
Open occasionally through the National
Gardens Scheme (see website for
further details: Broughton Poggs &
Filkins Gardens)
www.ngs.org.uk

Painswick Rococo Garden 1770
Painswick, Stroud
Open daily, Jan to Oct, 11am to 5pm
www.rococogarden.org.uk

Westbury Court Garden 1705
Westbury-on-Severn
Open Mar to Jun & Sep to Oct, Wed to
Sun, 10am to 5pm; open daily, Jul to
Aug, 10am to 5pm; open Bank Holiday
Mondays and other times by
appointment
www.nationaltrust.org.uk

**Westonbirt, The National
Arboretum** 1829
Tetbury
Open daily, Mon to Fri, 9am;
Sat & Sun, 8am
Closed 5pm (or dusk) during Dec to
Mar; 8pm (or dusk) during Apr to Nov
www.forestry.gov.uk

Hampshire

**Mottisfont Abbey Garden, House &
Estate** 1972
Mottisfont, Romsey
Garden open Mar to Oct, Sat to Thurs,
11pm to 5pm; Nov to Dec, Sat & Sun,
11am to 4pm; see website for
additional opening times during Mar
to Oct
www.nationaltrust.org.uk

Herefordshire

The Laskett 1974
Much Birch, Hereford
Occasional tours organized by Border
Lines; occasional open days organized
by Perennial (Gardeners' Royal
Benevolent Society)
www.border-lines.co.uk
www.perennial.org.uk

Hertfordshire

Hatfield House 1977
Hatfield
Park and West Garden open daily,
Mar to Sep, 11am to 5.30pm
East Garden open Mar to Sep, Thurs,
11am to 5.30pm
www.hatfield-house.co.uk

Isles of Scilly

Tresco Abbey Garden 1834
Tresco
Open daily, 10am to 4pm
www.tresco.co.uk

Kent

Godinton House & Gardens 1902
Ashford
Gardens open Mar to Oct, Thurs
to Mon, 2pm to 5.30pm
www.godinton-house-gardens.co.uk

Scotney Castle 1836
Lamberhurst, Tunbridge Wells
Open Mar, Sat & Sun, 11am to 4.30pm;
Mar to Nov, Wed to Sun, 11am to
5.30pm; Nov to Dec, Sat & Sun,
11am to 4pm
www.nationaltrust.org.uk

Port Lympne Gardens 1921
Port Lympne Wild Animal Park,
Lympne, Hythe
Open daily, 10am to 5pm; restricted
access during events
(see website for further details)
Closed Christmas Day
www.totallywild.net

Sissinghurst Castle Garden 1938
Sissinghurst, Cranbrook
Garden open Mar to Nov, Mon & Tues,
Fri to Sun, 11am to 6.30pm; open from
10am at weekends and Bank Holidays
www.nationaltrust.org.uk

London

Alexander Pope's Grotto 1744
St James Independent School for
Senior Boys, Pope's Villa, Twickenham,
Middlesex
Open for one week during summer;
tours by appointment (see website
for further details)
www.twickenham-museum.org.uk

Chelsea Flower Show
Royal Hospital, Chelsea
Annual event, see website for details
www.rhs.org.uk/chelsea

Chelsea Physic Garden 1722
Royal Hospital Road, Chelsea
Open Mar to Oct, Wed to Fri, 12pm
to 5pm; Sun, Bank Holidays & Good
Friday, 12pm to 6pm; Jul & Aug,
Wed, 12pm to 10pm
www.chelseaphysicgarden.co.uk

Chiswick House & Gardens 1725
Chiswick
Gardens open daily, 7am to dusk
www.chgt.org.uk

Myddelton House Gardens 1895
Enfield, Middlesex
Open Apr to Sep, Mon to Fri, 10am
to 4.30pm; Oct to Mar, Mon to Fri,
10am to 3pm; also open Easter to
Oct, Sun & Bank Holiday Mondays,
12pm to 4pm
Closed Christmas week & other
Bank Holidays
www.leevalleypark.org.uk

Strawberry Hill 1776
St Mary's University College,
Strawberry Hill, Twickenham, Middlesex
Public tours, Mar to Aug, Sun, 2pm,
2.45pm, 3.30pm; private tours by
appointment (see website for
further details)
www.friendsofstrawberryhill.org

Norfolk

East Ruston Old Vicarage 1980s
East Ruston, Norwich
Open Mar to Oct, Wed, Fri to Sun &
Bank Holidays, 2pm to 5.30pm; guided
tours and other events (see website

for further details)
www.e-ruston-oldvicaragegardens.co.uk

Holkham Hall 1872
Wells-next-the-sea
Park open daily, Easter to Oct, Mon
to Sat, 7am to 7pm; Sun, 9am to 7pm;
Oct to Easter, Mon, Wed & Fri, 7am
to 7pm; Tues & Thurs, 10am to 7pm;
weekends, pedestrian access only
Terraces around the Hall open Jun
to Sep, Mon to Thurs (excluding Bank
Holiday Mondays)
www.holkham.co.uk

Pensthorpe 2000
Pensthorpe Waterfowl Park,
Pensthorpe, Fakenham
Open daily, Apr to Dec, 10am to 5pm;
Jan to Mar, 10am to 4pm
Closed Christmas Day & Boxing Day
www.pensthorpe.com

Sheringham Park 1812
Upper Sheringham
Park open daily, dawn to dusk
www.nationaltrust.org.uk

North Yorkshire

Castle Howard 1720s
York
Gardens open daily, 10am to
6.30pm (dusk in winter)
Closed Christmas Day
www.castlehoward.co.uk

Rievaulx Terrace & Temples 1758
Rievaulx, Helmsley
Open daily, Mar to Sep, 11am to
6pm; Oct to Nov, 11am to 5pm
Ionic Temple closed 1pm to 2pm
www.nationaltrust.org.uk

Studley Royal 1742
Fountains Abbey & Studley Royal
Water Garden, Ripon, Harrogate
Open daily, Mar to Oct, 10am to 5pm
(or dusk); Nov to Feb, 10am to 4pm
(or dusk)
Closed Fridays in Nov to Jan,
Christmas Eve and Christmas Day
www.fountainsabbey.org.uk

Northumberland

Belsay Hall, Castle & Gardens
1870s
Belsay, Ponteland
Open daily, Mar to Sep, 10am to 5pm
and Oct, 10am to 4pm; open Nov to
Mar, Thurs to Mon, 10am to 4pm
Closed Christmas Eve, Christmas Day,
Boxing Day & New Year's Day
www.english-heritage.org.uk

Oxfordshire

Blenheim Palace 1774
Woodstock
Formal Gardens open daily, Feb
to Nov, 10am to 5.30pm; Nov to Dec,
Wed to Sun, 10am to 5.30pm
Park & Pleasure Gardens open daily
(except Christmas Day), 9am
to 5.30pm
www.blenheimpalace.com

Rousham House and Garden 1738
Steeple Aston, Bicester
Gardens open daily, 10am to 4.30pm
www.rousham.org

Shropshire

Hawkstone Park 1795
Weston-under-Redcastle, Shrewsbury
Open daily, Feb to Nov (see website for
opening times)
Open New Year's Day, 10am to 2.30pm
Closed Nov to Dec, except for Santa's
Grotto (see website for further details:
Hawkstone Park Follies)
www.hawkstone.co.uk

Somerset

East Lambrook Manor Gardens
1938
South Petherton
Open daily, 10am to 5pm
www.eastlambrook.co.uk

Montacute House 1590
Montacute, Yeovil
Garden open Mar, Wed to Sun, 11am
to 4pm; Mar to Nov, Wed to Mon, 11am
to 6pm; Nov to Dec, Wed to Sun, 11am
to 4pm
Park open daily
www.nationaltrust.org.uk

Staffordshire

Alton Towers 1814
Alton
Open daily, Mar to Nov, 9.30am
(see website for further details)
www.altontowersheritage.com

Biddulph Grange Garden 1850s
Biddulph
Open Mar, Sat & Sun, 11am to 4pm;
Mar to Nov, Wed to Sun, 11am to 5pm;
Nov to Dec, Sat & Sun, 11am to 3pm
Open Bank Holiday Mondays
www.nationaltrust.org.uk

Surrey

Claremont Landscape Garden 1715
Esher
Garden open, Feb to Mar, Tues to Sun,
10am to 5pm; Apr to Oct, daily, 10am
to 6pm; Nov to Jan, Tues to Sun, 10am
to 5pm
www.nationaltrust.org.uk

Hampton Court Palace 1699
East Molesey
Formal Gardens open daily,
Mar to Oct, 10am to 7pm; Oct to Mar,
10am to 5.30pm
Informal Gardens open daily,
Mar to Oct, 7am to 8pm; Oct to Mar,
7am to 6pm
Home Park open daily, Mar & Oct, 7am
to 6.45pm; Apr to Sep, 7am to 9pm;
Nov to Feb, 7am to 5.30pm
www.hrp.org.uk

Munstead Wood Garden 1897
Busbridge, Goldaming
Open occasionally through the National
Gardens Scheme (see website for
further details)
www.ngs.org.uk

Painshill Park 1773
Cobham
Open daily, Mar to Oct, 10.30am to
6pm (or dusk); Nov to Feb, 10.30am
to 4pm (or dusk)
Closed Christmas Day & Boxing Day
www.painshill.co.uk

Royal Botanic Gardens, Kew 1757
Kew, Richmond
Gardens open daily, Mar to Aug,
9.30am to 6.30pm weekdays & 7.30pm
weekends; Aug to Oct, 9.30am to 6pm
www.kew.org

Sutton Place 1986
Sutton Park, Sutton Green,
Guildford GU4 7QN
Open only by appointment for pre-
booked parties

West Midlands

The Leasowes 1763
Halesowen
Open daily, dawn to dusk
www.dudley.gov.uk

Wightwick Manor 1887
Wightwick Bank, Wolverhampton
Open Mar to Aug, Wed to Sat, 11am to
5pm; Aug, Wed to Sun, 11am to 5pm;
Sep to Dec, Wed to Sat, 11am to 5pm
www.nationaltrust.org.uk

West Sussex

Denmans 1980
Fontwell
Open daily, 9am to 5pm (or dusk)
www.denmans-garden.co.uk

Gravetye Manor 1885
East Grinstead
Now a hotel, gardens open
to hotel guests
www.gravetyemanor.co.uk

West Yorkshire

Bramham Park 1731
Wetherby
Grounds open daily, Mar to Sep,
11.30am to 4.30pm; but closed
during summer events (see website
for further details)
www.bramhampark.co.uk

Harewood House 1844
Harewood, Leeds
Grounds & gardens open daily,
Mar to Nov, 10am to 6pm
www.harewood.org

Wiltshire

The Peto Garden at Iford Manor
1899
Bradford-on-Avon
Open Easter Mon & Sun, 2pm to 5pm;
Apr & Oct, Sun, 2pm to 5pm;
May to Sep, Tues to Thurs, Sat & Sun,
2pm to 5pm
www.ifordmanor.co.uk

Stourhead 1740s
Stourton, Warminster
Garden open daily, 9am to 7pm
www.nationaltrust.org.uk

Wilton House 1635
Wilton, Salisbury
Grounds open Easter weekend,
11am to 5.30pm; Apr to Sep, 11am
to 5.30pm
www.wiltonhouse.co.uk

Worcestershire

Hanbury Hall 1701
Hanbury, Droitwich Spa
Garden and park open Mar, Sat & Sun,
11am to 5.30pm; Mar to Jun, Mon to
Wed, Sat & Sun, 11am to 5.30pm;
Jul to Aug, daily, 11am to 5.30pm;
Sep to Oct, Mon to Wed, Sat & Sun,
11am to 5.30pm; Nov to Jan, Sat &
Sun, 11am to 5.30pm; also Boxing Day
to New Year's Day, 11am to 5.30pm
www.nationaltrust.org.uk

Index

The entries in **bold** are the garden-makers and gardens featured in this book.

Acknowledgements

Texts written by Iona Baird, Guy Cooper, Aulani Mulford, Toby Musgrave, Jennifer Potter, Tim Richardson, Barbara Simms and Gordon Taylor.

Phaidon Press Limited
Regent's Wharf
All Saints Street
London N1 9PA

Phaidon Press Inc.
180 Varick Street
New York, NY 10014

www.phaidon.com

First published as *The Garden
Book* 2000
This edition abridged, revised and
updated 2008
© 2000, 2008 Phaidon Press Limited

ISBN 978 0 7148 4892 1

A CIP catalogue record for this book
is available from the British Library.

Designed by Susanne Olsson
Printed in China